MEN MOVED TO MARS

When Women Started Killing the Ones on Venus

A Humorous Approach to a Great Relationship

MIKE G. WILLIAMS
and TERICA L. WILLIAMS

Men Moved to Mars…When Women Started Killing the Ones on Venus: A Humorous Approach to a Great Relationship
Copyright ©2009 Mike G. Williams
All rights reserved

Cover Design by Pine Hill Graphics
Interior Design by Pine Hill Graphics

ISBN: 978-1-933150-17-8

Printed in the United States of America.

Table of Contents

About the Authors

Mike and Terica have been happily and consecutively married since 1983. They have four children and spend much of their life operating the Cups Of Cold Water Mission Project in the Dominican Republic. Before moving there Mike spent his days making audiences laugh all over the country and Terica led worship for a thriving church. Although the book was written in Mike's voice, we promise that Terica's input is imbedded in every page.

www . MikeWilliamsComedy . com

Other books by Mike G. Williams

Night Lights and Other Things That Save Toes 1990

Turkey Soup for the Sarcastic Soul 2003

More Turkey Soup for the More Sarcastic Soul 2005

Life Happens... Shut Up, Smile, And Get a Plunger 2007

An Amateurs Guide to Skunk Repair 2009

Love is Not a Three Letter Word 2012

Never Stand Under A Flock Of Angry Birds 2013

Awaken the Mighty Men 2015

Parable of the Muddy Jeep 2015

Introduction

When the Creator put Men and Women on earth together, I think it started out as a practical joke and simply got out of hand. Nevertheless here we are today! Let's just laugh and go with it.

This book is for those who are single and wish they were married... and for those who are married and wish they were single! Sorry. I meant to say for those who are married and desire to have a great relationship with their spouse. To be quite honest with you, I believe every person who has ever attended our marriage seminar says they wish that they had been told the information found in part 1 of this book before they ever started dating. They don't always say those nice comments about part 2 of this book. Part 2 can be a little blunt. A little in your face! I hope you like both parts.

> *Most Women are attracted to the simple things in life. Like Men.*
> *–Henny Youngman*

Let me start off by telling you this is not your normal relationship betterment book! I believe that "a better marriage" is not good enough. Good has always been the enemy of great. Who wants to go through life just a little better? Stephen Covey did not become a billionaire by giving you 7 Habits of Fairly Successful People! Who wants to see a good movie when you can see a great one? You wouldn't settle for an average restaurant when you could eat at the best one for the same price, or would you? Understand that it is the desire of this author to motivate you to desire the best in your marriage relationship and achieve it. Never settle for mediocrity.

> *Marriage has no guarantees. If that's what your looking for,*
> *go live with a car battery. –Erma Bombeck*

You should be told right now that this is not a remake of all the marriage books I have ever read. I can say that honestly because I have never read one. I have a few of them on my bookshelf, but like many other people who own a dark walnut credenza, I haven't read ten percent of the books on the shelves behind my desk. They are there to impress my clients into thinking that I am the most "well-read" person in the world. So if you ever see this book on your therapist's shelf... ask if he/she agreed with my first point about books on the dark walnut credenza shelf. If he/she stumbles or stutters, or says, "What do you mean by that?", you will know that he/she has not read it, confirming my observation. Their next question will most likely be, "How does that make you feel?" For the record, I do have strong intentions of going back and reading all the great books on this subject real soon. Next week. Tomorrow maybe. I do acknowledge there are some very-very good ones you need to read… but right after you finish this one.

Wives are people who think it's against the law to not answer a phone when it rings. –Rita Rudner

If any of those little sarcastic statements bothered you I would suggest that you put this book down right now and write your own book. There will be more. This book will take great liberties with humor for two reasons. The first is that I love to laugh. If you have ever spent any amount of time with me you know that there is going to be a lot of laughing throughout this book. It does not make any difference to me whether you are laughing at me or with me… let's have some laughs along with the read. Another reason laughter will be prevalent is that I believe if you want to keep contemporary brains (especially male brains) interested in a book you better have a little humor to break the tension that often comes when we talk about serious subjects. We will deal with some very heavy and very taboo subjects, but in a humorous way! I promise you that.

All Men are born free, but some get married. –E. C. Mckenzie

If you think that because you are already married that you need to skip the first section of this book, you would be very-very WRONG! Missing the axioms of the first section are the primary reason that messy marriages are messy, and lousy relationships are lousy. Skip these first chapters and you might as well just put this book on your shelf to impress your friends.

I've always wondered; should Women stay home and raise the children or should Men have to raise themselves –Paul Aldrich

It was somewhere in Texas where I met a Christian Psychologist who dropped a concept on me that I never forgot. He loosely said, "Many of my clients come to me for counseling, when all they really want to do is to be able to tell their friends and family that they are taking charge of their life, but they don't really want to change." Hmm… there is some interesting "ology" in that statement. Is he right? I don't know, I'm certainly not a Texas based Christian Psychologist. I will say this, though… If you are just reading the book so you can be one of "those" people, please return this book to the store you bought it at. I really don't care to waste my words on relationship tire kickers, but if you want a great marriage… read on. Was that overtly harsh for you? Get over it. The truth often hurts… wear some protective gear.

If I have learned one thing about Women it is this… I don't know much about Women! When they think I have learned a few things… they will change.

Let me confess that I am not a good counselor. I'm rather horrible at it, but I did stay at a Holiday Inn Express last night… that has got to count for something. I do spend a lot of time contemplating these issues in an effort to personally have a great marriage. I can testify to the fact that our second greatest foundational problem in marriage (I will give you the big one later) is as simple as miscommunication. We have a language problem. When I say that, I don't mean that we speak completely different languages.

It would be better described as the difference between South Georgia English and Bostonian English. The difference between synonyms and synonyms. Yes I meant to say synonyms twice! This miscommunication has led to a variety of problems!

> *When we first met my wife didn't like me that much.*
> *Luckily, she wanted to stay in this country. –Brian Kiley*

From the very beginning Men and Women have dealt with different understandings of the same word, different understandings of the same thought, and different understandings of the same ideas. In other words… We hear different things when the same thing is said. Don't feel bad though, from the time we were very young we were given different definitions for the same words.

> *Women don't want to hear what Men think. Women want to hear what they think in a deeper voice.*

There are Women sayings and Men sayings. There is "Ladies first"… compared to… "Every Man for himself". Women register for weddings and showers… Men register to buy a gun! Woman's best friend is a diamond… Mans best friend is a dog. Yes, Women's best friend takes thousands of years to create and is made from the rarest minerals on earth. A Mans best friend is available "FREE TO A GOOD HOME" on the local bulletin board. Now this in no way is intended to belittle Men or Women. It just means that though we speak the same words… we don't always speak the same language.

> *Marriage is a wonderful invention… then again…*
> *so is Cheeze Whiz! –Ken Lash*

Now I am not trying to use this introduction to excuse either of our language differences. Rather I seek to build a good case for the information and education I wish to expound upon in the coming chapters. So give me a break, sit back, and let me have an appetizer of fun before we delve into the main course.

> *You can't buy love, but you can pay heavily for it.*
> *–Henny Youngman*

Now some of you Ladies reading this book may find yourself appalled that Men cannot speak your language, and in fact some Men act as though they do not even care to speak it. For that I apologize for all males everywhere. Please understand that Men are born with a handicap. We are brain damaged from birth! It is not our fault… From our pre-natal days… When a little boy is in the womb… his brain is attacked by testosterone which kills 90% of our brain cells. After meeting a few of the male species of which I call myself a part of, I can't help but think that some of us may have lost an even higher percentage. We are lucky we can ever comprehend inhaling and exhaling, much less the intricacies of the female mind and emotion. Does this make me a male basher? No. I am proud to be a Man. Men will always rule the world… that is because the "world rulership" is currently and has always been controlled by upper body strength. Remember… Men are operating on 10%… right out of the gate. This is why we love NASCAR. This is why we can sit totally enthralled with cars going around the same circle hundreds of times and not notice that our two year old son has set fire to his sister's Barbie dolls on the floor in front of us. We may have given him the matches... we don't remember!

Things change. When I first got married I would walk around the house with no clothes on and my husband would say, "Baby you look so good." He couldn't keep his hands off of me. Now I walk around the house with no clothes on and he says, "Aint you cold.?" –Roz Browne

I have heard speakers attribute this "dilemma" to a self-esteem problem. Modern therapy does like to use self-esteem issues as a catch-all reason for every problem. Whatever! please consider that the male self esteem hit an all time low somewhere a few days after we were born when a doctor took a pair of scissors to our... our... special area! That has got to mess you up at any age. I think either gender could recognize that, aye? Think about this from another perspective. Let's go back to adolescence for a moment. Consider one of the very first rhymes we are taught.

Girls are are made of sugar and spice and everything nice

What are boys left with if the girls have "everything" nice? "Excuse me Teacher, what are boys made of?" The teacher now has a dumb look on her face. They have to come up with something. They can't just say, "Well we hadn't thought of that." So they quickly write a closing to the poem...

Boys are made of snippets and snails and puppy dog tails

I know snails. I know puppy dog tails. What are snippets? Throw in a dead cat and we are nothing more than the leftovers from a chinese restaurant that didn't pass the health inspection. Boys are chop-suey! All-You-Can-Eat of it too. Girls are a delicious dessert - guys are a leftover casserole. Again, this in no way is intended to belittle Men or Women. It just means that though we speak the same words... we come from a different culture and perspective.

Men and Women belong to different species, and communication between them is still in its infancy.

It is common knowledge that the public school teaching style (pedagogy) is best suited to teach girls. I believe this is why Women can talk and Men cannot! You want to know why Men can't carry on deep meaningful conversation? We don't know how! Most of our language skills are still in the dark ages. Listen to two young girls talking. "Oh I love your dress! That is the most beautiful lavender and lace blouse I have ever seen, where did you get it? Is that color plum, passionfruit or pomegranate?" The average guy can't spell pomegranate.... much less pick it out of a line-up of primary colors. Listen to a group of adolescent guys talking... if you want to call it talking. I believe it to be more like guttural noises than talking. "UUUH... d'jou see the game?" "UHU... good." "Uhh... go Patriots!" Again, this is why we like sports... "I got nothing to say... mmm... aaamm... Hey Bob... you go long for a pass!"

E-Harmony has done for dating - what CarMax has done for used car buying. Your match has been prescreened to see if they have any unseen frame damage or past wrecks. They have passed a thorough inspection, and you can view them, and even buy them online if you wish. Now that's what I call simple.

Men and Women go to the Bathroom differently. No… I'm not talking about the obvious! Men go one-at-a-time. Women go in groups of two or more. What do you do in there ladies that requires it to be a tag-team experience? When did nose powdering and flushing become a team sport? If a Man did strike up a real conversation with another Man in a restroom he would be kicked out of the Man Club! If it got around that a Man was having a conversation in the bathroom he would be thought of as… well you know. Hey we are not even allowed to tap our foot to the overhead music. You could get arrested for this in Minnesota… even if you're a Senator!

Never buy a Man a reading lamp that won't fit in his bathroom!

While we are in the bathroom, gaze into the shower for just a minute. What do you see? Women have 15 different shower items to gently wash off old skin, clean and moisturize the new skin, fix split ends, restore youthful color, bring back body and fullness, restore bounce and shine, and other items that help you to exfoliate. I don't even know what part of the body one would exfoliate or how one would do it. They never taught me that in shop class. Men have a three-in-one combination body wash, shampoo, and conditioner. It is also referred to by it's common name… Dishwashing Liquid.

90 percent of Men say the first thing they notice about Women is their eyes, while 90 percent of Women say these Men are big fat liars! Obviously the remaining 10 percent of Women were not available for the survey.

These Women's products are all natural health products made with things like papayas, coconuts, and rare fruits imported from exotic places like Fiji. Mens three-in-one body wash, shampoo, and conditioner is made out of Isopropyl alcohol, Recycled asbestos, and FD&C Yellow #6 imported from non-exotic places like a New Jersey landfill. Women's products could be used as a tasty salad dressing at fine restaurant. Mens products can also be used to control the rodent population at a fine restaurant.

Men are superior to Women. For one thing,
Men can urinate from a speeding car. –Will Durst

Look at our clothing differences. Women have a completely different wardrobe for every season. Men have a T-shirt for any occasion. There is nothing a Man needs in his wardrobe that couldn't be bought at Bass Pro Shops of America. Women have running accounts at the Dry Cleaners for careful care of various fabrics. A Man could wash any outfit he owns with a wet sponge and a spray bottle of Febreeze fabric freshener. Men have shoes. Women have heels, flats, sandals, stiletto's, slides, pumps, tennis, jogging, casuals, formals, and who knows what else? Each of these in various outfit matching colors. Again this in no way is intended to belittled Men or Women. It just expresses the concept that though we use the same language… we don't always speak the same version of that language.

Women aren't so hard to understand, they all just want to hear those three little words, "I was wrong." –Reno Goodale

A Woman has planned her wedding since she was five years old. She may even have a hope chest filled with special items and written plans for that ceremony. A guy wants to grow up to be a superhero and in the back of his mind thinks that it could somehow possibly happen. The guy may have hardly thought about asking her to marry him prior to asking… and that was by accident. He meant to say… "I forgot my wallet… Will you carry me?" That's why he was on one knee… he was looking for spare change under the table to pay the check.

A study in the Washington Post says that Women have better verbal skills than Men. I just want to say to the authors of that study, "Duh!"
–Conan O'Brien

I believe it was fourth grade vocabulary that taught me the word "bride" is taken from the latin and is a word used to denote beauty and grace. The word "groom" was originally used in 1667 to denote a male in charge of cleaning a stable. You don't even have to be smarter than a fifth grader to see this little inequity. I believe the word "groom" is used to remind the Man to shower and shave the morning of his wedding. All the wedding gifts are for the Women. The Man doesn't really need appliances, linen, and fancy underwear. A Man could live comfortably buck-naked in a Airstream camper as long as he had a fishing pole, a shotgun, and a good BBQ grill to cook on. Oh yes… and a similarly dressed female counterpart.

Men like to barbecue. Men will cook if danger is involved.
–Rita Rudner

So you see that both sexes are genetically encoded to be different from day one! Nevertheless much of our life is spent trying to get the other sex to look our way, be pleased, and thus investigate. That is good. That is adventure! If you see a relationship as a journey, this road will excite you. I love my wife, though I struggle to understand her dialect. Nevertheless she has been nothing shy of a great adventure. She is my intriguing foreign lover.

Many of my friends are getting married and buying diamonds for their fian-cées. What a better way to symbolize a marriage than with the hardest thing known to Man. –Mike Dugan

Just so you will know Ladies… Mars Man has always been a fantasizer. Those Men who saw some of their great fantasies come true were called Visionaries and Explorers. Please remember it all started with a fantasy! You can call it a dream, or call it a vision, but that is just a high-brow name for fantasy. Men can combine fantasies, dreams, and visions! Men have the ability to envision developing a beef-jerky flavored cheese that is both all-natural and squeezable from a toothpaste style dispenser. They dream about owning a vintage Harley Davidson motorcycle. They fantasize about making whoopee on the deck of the now infamous S.S. Minnow! Mars Man can even combine his fantasy to include the Harley and the squeeze-cheese and the whoopee on the deck of the S.S. Minnow together in the same daydream! I saw the poster once!

My girlfriend is not a ball and chain—
she's more of a spring-loaded trap. –Kevin Hench

The internet dating sites promise to somehow match you on a billion levels of compatibility. Yeah, thats funny! LOL! What about the rest of us who are already legally married or at least emotionally connected to someone who does not match us on those billion levels of compatibility? Terica and I would be lucky to match on three points, and one of those is rather insignificant. I wouldn't call the fact that we both like mushroom pizza and also use a blow dryer a dynamic match point! What about those singles who have looked through the E-Harmonious online options and still find themselves coming up a little E-missing? Or what about those who found themselves rejected as possible candidates by the very sites that made those braggadocios promises? Well this book offers hope to all of us. In fact this book dares to proclaim there is more than hope... there are miracles awaiting you! You need to be assured that you can have a great marriage. By the way (pay attention English majors), I most often capitalize Man, Woman, Men, Women (and the like) for the sake of showing each group the respect they really do deserve. We are in a generation that has lost respect for its sexual counterpart. This is my way of turning the tide. If that bothers you... get over it. It's my book... I will write the way I desire!

Quid Pro Quo!

Can everyone have a great marriage? I can't speak for everyone... but you can! I mean it! It can be achieved. The mediocrity myth is over. The truth is out. The cover has been blown. The banner has been lifted. The white smoke has puffed from the papal chimney! Okay that last one didn't make any sense, sorry! Without a doubt we know that there are people... on this planet... who have great marriages. So it is doable. It is achievable... for you.

I think they should use children's books to prepare children for real life.
"See Dick acting like a moron. See Jane becoming somehow emotionally
dependent to this loser. Jane thinks she can change him. Run, Jane, run!"

Now go get a cup of coffee and start reading the good parts of this book. Because whether you are a Man or Woman, if you think that what I wrote above is a synopsis of this book... trust me... You aint read nothing yet. Get ready to laugh. chuckle, agree, be appalled, offended, shocked, stunned, moved, broken, and most hopefully fixed! Was that statement too much? My desire is to see you have a great marriage and for singles to have a great relationships on your way to the altar. This is not rocket science... but it is brain surgery. So lean back and start counting backwards from one-hundred.

The older you get the lower your standards get. I used to be so picky. Oh,
when I get married he's going to be tall, handsome, rich...and I'm down to:
registered voter. I'd marry a midget just for the handicapped parking.
–Kathleen Madigan

For all Mars Men and Venus Women: This book is divided into two parts. The first being what I consider the foundational systems of a great relationship (bond) and secondly, the maintenance and or fulfillment of a great relationship (bond). Most of the couples I have worked with who are struggling to have a great marriage discover that their foundation has had some problems from the beginning. If you start with an unstable foundation you will never be able to get the walls of a house to be level. You will spend your life trying to get the doors to close right and the windows to simply open. So please be sure to read and understand Part One of this book first. It will make the make over so much easier.

1.0

HOW THE VENUS VIOLENCE STARTED

I wonder what sort of a tale we've fallen into? But I don't know. And that's the way of a real tale. Take any one that you're fond of.
–J. R. R. Tolkien, The Lord of the Rings

Should I start this chapter out like a story? A story always keeps interest and there is usually always a happy ending. Yes the *Prince* always gets his *Princess*... and vice versa. So without further adieu... I present to you a tale of two people, two entities, two aliens, two diametrically opposed fronts... well you get the point. Here we go.

Once upon a time Man found himself alone. Though there were many creatures, great and small around him, and he could find companionship, he needed more. That's when he thought to himself, "I will build a rocket ship and go cruise the galaxy looking for chicks!" He was in for a pleasant surprise!

At the same time Women on Venus decided to build a rocket ship to explore the galaxy in hopes of finding a *Super Wal-Mart* or at least the galaxy's largest *Outlet Mall* they could explore. As fate would have it, both spacecraft mysteriously landed on planet Earth. *Men landed here accidentally because they would not stop and ask for directions to the planet they intended to visit and Women because they needed to stop off for a restroom break.* Man, finding the Venus Woman rather attractive, and due to his impulsive nature, asked a Venus Girl to go for ride in his land rover. These Venus girls were rather beautiful and shapely... very different from him. They frolicked and played, and shared dreams and ideas. They marveled in each others differences and appreciated them, even if for nothing more than explorative interest. Well somewhere during the trip Mars Man ran out of gas, and due to the fact that there was no towing service available they decided to unite and set up a little house on the prairie.

From that point on a battle began. Venus Lady spent the next forty years trying to change Man into a Venustonian and Mars Man spent the next eight thousand years hiding in his garage secretly trying to rebuild his rusted spacecraft to return to Mars. Certainly he had forgotten how lonely he was on Mars, but the pressure on Earth to be Venustonian was more than he bargained for. Mars Man started out wanting to take a Venus Lady to Denny's for supper and a movie... and now there are three kids, diapers to buy, a factory job at her dad's plant, a big mortgage on a big dream home from a dream he never had, and an I-Pod. *Okay that was a little misleading, but with literary license, hopefully it has over cast a shadow of interest to what kinda' happened in the Garden of Eden.*

Venus is one of the hottest planets in our solar system... 900 degrees at the surface. This explains why Women on earth are always cold. I'll bet there are Women on Venus... at 900 degrees who still carry a sweater!

Go back to Genesis Chapter two for a moment. Here we find Adam meandering about the garden. He swings from the vines and roars with the lions... a regular *Tarzan* type chap for sure, *but without a loin cloth!* The Creator decides that it is not good for this guy to be alone. Maybe the Creator realized what a screw-up this guy would be on his own? This fellow might never do laundry. *Not that there was any laundry to do.* This fellow might never do dishes. This fellow might never put a new roll of toilet paper onto the roll, much less put the seat down. *In fact he would more than likely just pee on the seat and forget about it.* So the Creator parades all the animals before Adam and asks him to pick out a mate. Adam miraculously doesn't settle for a fish, or a deer, or a hunting dog, or a monkey. He didn't even settle for a kangaroo or an opossum. *Whereas I was sure he would have gravitated toward a marsupial.* Oh boy... What are we going to do? Before long Man finds himself napping the afternoon away next to a shady tree on the grassy ground, the same ground from which he came. The Creator chooses to perform a surgery and remove a bone from his side. *Be aware that this was done [apparently] without permission!* From his side the Creator takes a rib which became the building block for all of Womankind. *I knew there was a reason I like B.B.Q. ribs!* Not from the dirt like Adam, but from the side. There are many *poetic illustrations* I could give for why it was the *side* and not the *head*, and the *side* and not the *foot*, and the *side* and not the *ear*, but that would be nothing more than poetic license and speculative homilies and those are best utilized to extend the length of a marriage ceremony. Needless to say Man wakes from his *birthing sleep* to find Eve. A famous comedian says of female creation, "God saw this was a good thing...and Man saw it was a good thing...and God said... 'WO...MAN!'" Adam replied, "Bone of my bone, and flesh of my flesh..." It was as if he had been trapped on a deserted island for his entire life and then finds another lonely castaway... and she speaks his language... sort of. If it had been me I would have said something really profound like, "Daddy like," or "Hubba-hubba!"

Marriage is the only war where you sleep with the enemy.
–MS Magazine

As I now research it, and also by the general consensus of greater minds than I, you can only conclude that Woman became the refiner of Man. She became what was needed to finesse him. To make him acceptable to the human race. To teach him enough etiquette that he could be taken out to a fancy restaurant and not eat with his hands! Since that time there has been a problem... rebellious Man has fought to remain the Hunter, the Tarzan, the space explorer, the wild Lion! Man has fought to retain his position as king of the food chain and not succumb to these feministic tendencies toward frilly, fancy, and shiny. His absolute delight in female companion-ship has caused him to sell his spacecraft and pay for a stainless steel double door refrigerator, but there is still the desire for space travel in him. Woman has raised the whip and the chair in an attempt to tame the lion! She has dressed him up in designer clothes, but underneath the cumber bun and coat is a mangy coat of hair that needs a shampoo. Badly!

Adam had it easy. He was alone and God created the perfect Woman for him. God says, "It is not good for this guy to be by himself... he needs somebody to keep him in touch with reality... I will help him out." At no point in Genesis do you find Adam at a singles Bar looking for a hot chick or two or three. There was no Elimidate... no E-Harmony... no Internet... heck, there were no options! There was no singles scene, no personal ads, no first date, no dating process, no bad dates, no psycho chicks who stalk you, or call you for the next five years and you have to get a restraining order for... but let's not bring my life into Adam's scenario! If Adam was somehow transported into the 21st century, I wonder what his personals add would have looked like. Instead of "Single White Male," it would have read "Only Male, outdoor type, great with animals, likes gardening, loves laying around and eating fruit, Loves to take long walks in the Garden, seeking a perfect mate. Seeking mate who feels as if they are a part of me. Seeking a soul mate... bone of my bone - flesh of flesh type of relationship."

Gunther Gebel Williams was and is perhaps the most famous lion trainer ever known. He stated, "You can train a lion, but you can never tame one." Historic writ has an obscure passage that depending on the version you read from, talks of the Woman's task with Man being that of taming/training a wild lion! Yes... Women are lion *trainers* trying to be lion *tamers,* trying to do a job that cannot be done! We Men will always be barely a few dozen I.Q. points above potty-trained lions. Yes we might dress up, and even wear deodorant... but at some point we are going to roar if for nothing more that to express our macho image as King of the Garden! Women, in general would do well to understand that they have made great strides with Men in just getting us to occasionally comb our miens and wash between our claws. *You might want to read about Sigfried and Roy's journey in training/taming lions. How did that work out?* In fact I want to declare that "taming" will never happen. You may train Men, but taming... never! Unless bred in total captivity, Men for the most part will be Men. They will tend toward rough, rugged, ruthless, maniacal, insecure, boisterous, egotistical, and lovers of things done in dirt. Is it any wonder we like hunting, fishing, dirt bike riding, and just plain getting dirty. We like mud-wrestling! Men are hunters in search of everything, including a doe. It is our nature to return to where we were created. As for reinventing Women... maybe I will save that for a chapter by itself.

If a Lady has a bad attitude all the time could you justifiably call it habitual? Pardon the pronunciation. I'm just asking a question. –Robert G. Lee

Have you ever looked at a *young couple in love* and wondered about the outcome of this *so-called* union made in heaven? I could write an entire chapter on those relationships that anyone with half a brian knew would be nothing more than a blatant shipwreck. How many girls have had a list of animal traits attached to their boyfriend by family and friends? The list goes on and on. *He's lazy, he drinks too much, he's got a rap sheet longer than Al Capone, and… he still lives with his mother!* Now this list of offensivities is met with the same flippant response, "I can change him!" Oh yeah… your love, which has not accomplished transformation so far other than to get him to occasionally cut back from unfiltered regulars to menthol lights is going to turn that puppy around with the flip of his lighter on the unity candle. *Sure! Whatever.* Okay, I'm sounding a little sarcastic. Let me move on… but remember what you know about the training and or taming of lions. Then again, love is blind, and often deaf and dumb to boot!

***I wish people would learn to love me for who I am
pretending to be… this week.***

To thine own self be true. You have to be yourself. Those are statements I have heard for years. *What a crock!* We have *all* become influenced by our surroundings. To say that we are remaining true to our own self is to actually say that we are remaining true to the input we have been given by past culture. We all have been erroneously affected by secular peer pressure. Thus, we should be a little less self-affirming and realize that throughout our Christian life we *are called* to be personally morphing. As a Christ follower I am doing my best to let *Him* influence my life and change me from the inside out every day. So with that in mind we ought to all be a little more changeable *for the better*, right?

For Mars Man: Understand that this reprogramming is actually good for you. Left to yourself you would do nothing but kill and be killed. This delicate flower known as Woman is the best thing to happen since the invention of front fly cotton loin cloth! Let's learn to appreciate the education and cultural expedition we are experiencing. Dig deep into the hunter-gatherer-explorer genes that are buried under that leather skin and let's have an adventure with this female.

For Venus Woman: The fact that you are a Woman has forced you into the animal training business. Sorry. Take it up with God when you see Him. Now certainly you could forsake your natural affinity to straighten the crooked and calm the crazed, but that would be denying who you are. Embrace your challenge with vigor and realize it isn't always easy. Some trainers get eaten by the very lions thy feed. It happens. Again, sorry. Hey, we are eternal beings, quit living like you are not. Seeing yourself as an eternal being puts time and most issues into proper perspective. Be careful not to over-morph this guy. Your attraction to him is based on his being rather different. We will talk more about this real soon.

1.1

ANTENNAE CLIPPING WON'T MAKE A MARTIAN NORMAL

Don't ask what marriage can do for you... ask what you can do for your marriage

Many years ago I was speaking at a conference with Tony Campolo. Who doesn't love this guy? Working with Tony is truly an experience. It is like working with a combination of a potty-trained monkey and a wild donkey (I think he is a Democrat) with a semi-theological bent. So as sweat poured down his shiny scalp, Tony ranted (as he usually does) about the audacity of a national newspaper describing the physical beauty of a Miss America by printing her actual body measurements next to her picture. "Oh the audacity," Tony screamed, "To rate a Woman by the size of her private body parts!" He looked down at me. *This is not good to be spotted by Tony.* He said, "Mike! How would you like it... if the USA Today paper showed your picture and proclaimed... Mike - Nine Inches?" The crowd roared and I climbed under the seat. He went on to address an interesting idea that has spoken to me many times since that embarrassing day. He argued that most Men and Women get married because they are looking for someone to come along side of them and fill all the voids in their own life. They are looking for someone to bring to their marital table what they could not seem to find in their singleness. They are looking for an outsider to bring the inner person whatever they think they need in their life. His message challenged these singles (it was a singles conference we were both speaking at) to become a whole (complete) person before entering into marriage, for to enter marriage without being whole was tantamount to bringing certain destruction to a relationship. "Unhealthy people will kill each other trying to get the other person to make them feel healthy, and it won't work," Tony proclaimed. Unhealthy people will not become healthy by linking with other unhealthy people. Two plus two will never equal ten. It was a great message! I certainly know that I have put my wife through much turmoil trying to make her be what I thought would make me feel happy and fulfilled. It didn't work, it doesn't work, and it won't start working in the near future. So maybe we need to try another way.

How do you get a Man to change out a roll of empty toilet paper? Who knows how you get a Man to change anything?
–Chonda Pierce

It was concepts like these and others that led me on this literary journey. I am not a licensed Physician. I am not a Psychologist, Psychiatrist, Therapist, or licensed marriage counselor. I carry no degree in any field related to marriage or personal development. Yet, after being told that most professionals have less than a 10% success rate in fixing marriages, I feel like I am overqualified. In the multiple decades of my wife and I being married, we have spent a few hours with a counselor. *Truthfully these were usually friends of ours who were in the counseling business, because I am too cheap to actually pay for a shrink.* Most of the counseling was a waste of time as it focused on how I needed to change! We can all guess how well I took to that. *Do Men ever change?* Most people push for counseling… in hopes that a neutral party will tell their spouse that he or she needs to "straighten up" or "correct their ways!" Sometimes our little impromptu sessions from our well meaning friends even focused on what she needed to change. I applaud that! *She needs to change!* With a few changes our life together could be *better*. Some of those I have counseled would be content if their counseling turned out to produce a tolerable relationship. Tolerable? *Tolerable aint good!* I hate better, when best is an option.

> ### As a Man I look forward to continued immaturity followed by death. –Dave Barry

So maybe we had been missing something. Maybe that little rather insignificant statement back at the singles conference contained some deep truth. Truth that says boldly, "I need to stop trying to change my spouse and start working to achieve wholeness in my own heart first." Let's not just stop there though, because there is a lot more that I learned and you certainly wouldn't want to pay the price of this book for me to spill most of the good answers in the first few pages. Consequently the journey begins for you where it has ended this week for me. So read on.

> ### Do I believe that individuals can be 100% whole and sane? Yes… but rarely. Consequently… we need to be more spiritually and emotionally whole than we are sick if we are going to live in the same house.

Remember that I have never read a marriage book. I must go on to confess that I cannot remember most of what I was supposed to do from the counseling sessions. What I share comes from my understanding of the Word of God and many years of marriage… many of those very happy years… especially the most recent ones. Both this book and our corresponding *Great Marriage Weekend* seminar is designed to help you laugh and learn how to attain a great marriage. I pray it will. *If not you might want a refund and I have already spent the publishers forward on a new flat panel television. You know… the ones that damage the ozone layer? Yes, I thought our household had gone green until I found out about the ozone damaging flat-screens. So in light of that, I'm going green - tomorrow.*

> ### Marriage is very difficult. Marriage is like a 5,000-piece jigsaw puzzle—all sky. –Cathy Ladman

So as you start this book… stop for a minute! This is not a quick fix book for your bad marriage or bad marriage to come. It is a humorous little dissertation that calls us all back to the basics and dares to ask the questions that nobody ever asked me. Again, the humor is not for the faint of heart or weak of funny bone. The many comedians we've quoted here were speaking out of their own life experiences and we will have to take it at that. Enjoy. Laugh. Live. Journey! I am reminded of the story that Jeff Allen told me a few months ago. Apparently someone bought one of his DVD's and was not pleased with the jokes and humorous stories contained within it. This person, called Jeff's home phone at eight in the morning to complain that she didn't like the comedy or the sarcasm. I believe Jeff's wife fielded the call and responded by suggesting that Jeff might have been better if he had "Sold her a sense of humor instead of a DVD!" Please take the point to heart and laugh along as you read.

Men take four billion sperm to get a one egg fertilized? This is because no part of a Man will ever stop and ask for directions.

Be aware that this book and its corresponding seminar is going to make some generalizations that may not be exacting to every marital situation or every personality type. People are different. *Some people would consider it an insult to be asked to be on a Jerry Springer Show... and others would consider it an honor.* Some will find that their own personalities lay in what is in direct opposite to the norm... and that is alright. Read the book anyway. I fully understand that not all relationships contain a Woman who is the dominant conversationalist. Not all relationships contain a Man who has a greater sex drive than his spouse! Not all Men are bad listeners. Not all Women are terrible gripes! Not every Man is only thinking about sex. *Not all Women put on makeup in the car at a green light and hold up traffic!* Not every Man and every Woman has a bad mother-in-law! *Not all Men refuse to take out the trash... there is that one guy in northeast Minnesota who actually enjoys it.*

Not all Women abhor sex! In fact very few do. The ones who do are usually the unfortunate victims of some type of early predator type behavior. That breaks my heart. Please do not use the minority to speak for the majority.

Let me let you in on something. My dear spouse struggles with negative comedy that often stereotypes the Woman and the Man. She has been helping me edit my comedy for years, and would definitely *cut some* jokes that I wouldn't. Marital stereotypes run the gamut of extreme when exemplified by comedians. Most comedians portray Men as sex crazed beings that married Women whom are less interested in sex than they are interested in how to make catfish bait out of an old tube sock. My dear spouse would declare strongly that many Women happen to enjoy sex as much as Men. More on that topic later. *I will let the jokes stand as they are.*

Now as I mentioned at the close of the introduction, before we can begin our foray into the world of our marriage we will have to take a trip back to our dating life (the number 1 foundational problem). You may think that this has little to do with your marriage. *Oh my misguided friend!* Allow me to suggest that your dating practices virtually dictated your marital happiness often long before you even met your spouse (or future spouse). Let us go back to dating 101. Let us look at a Biblically based, unmentioned-unmentionable from scripture. Yes, we will look into the times when, and reasons why, religious leadership actually required the couple to have sex before they were even married. *You can see why this particular incident is not preached that often in Sunday morning Youth class!* Nevertheless the foundational material found in the first few chapters of this book will set the foundation for all we discuss. So if you are married or plan on getting married sometime before you leave this Earth… you need to grab another cup of caffeine and keep reading.

I will close this introductory chapter with the verses you will never hear read at a wedding unless I am doing the ceremony. *Well maybe other Ministers do it too… I don't have quantifiable data on that subject.* If I am there I will make sure you have the entire truth on the issue. I will not be one of these liberal Pastors who do marriages for the fifty dollar untaxed gift certificate and walk away. I charge twenty-five dollars and I pay tax on it! *I am legally allowed to marry people because I am a notary!* Anyway, here are the verses you will hear me quote…

It is good for a Man not to marry. –1 Corinthians 7:1b (NIV)

But those who marry will face many troubles in this life, and I want to spare you this. –1 Corinthians 7:28b (NIV)

For the record, I also read many other nice Bible verses too. I also read the entire lyrics to Don Henley's song *For My Wedding* and much of his song *Heart of The Matter.* My ceremony can take up to ten minutes if I get wordy. I have done entire wedding ceremonies that were less than five minutes. People who arrived late got to watch the rice being thrown. *You can hardly afford to throw rice anymore… what with the shortages and all!* For the record I refuse to do any wedding where they are playing or singing the song *There Is Love.* I hate that song. Is there a wedding rule that requires us to have somebody signing it who sounds like a cat in a blender? I'm just asking. *By the way, I have never actually heard a real cat in a real blender… I am just imagining.*

For Mars Man: Can you commit the time it takes to make a great relationship? Or will you settle for second rate slop all your life? It takes time to make a good meal. Throw your microwave away. Look, you could have chosen the single life. You could have become a monk. Throwing caution to the wind you said, "No… I must have a Woman! I need a Woman." So seeing that your very internal desires lead you in this direction… take the time to get it right.

For Venus Woman: I could reword what I just said for you, but I won't. Just read what I wrote to the Mars Man and apply it to a female gender. Be glad that modern customs do not require you to share him. Although I think that may be why Men had multiple Wives. It might have taken a team effort to train primitive Mars Man. Who knows? *I'm not for this at all, though I did type this chapter while waiting on a airplane at the Salt Lake City Airport.*

1.2

SPACE EXPLORATION GAVE US VELCRO

Do you ever read those singles ads or watch the dating commercials and think to yourself... Oh those poor misguided souls? Bless their hearts!

All I know is that some scientist fellow found that some types of weeds cling to clothes by what they refer to as a *hook and loop* principle. This hook and loop discovery was apparently developed further by N.A.S.A. to improve space travel. I have no idea how it was used. I just know that I was taught as a kid to respect the space program because it gave us innovations like Velcro. I still have an old Velcro wallet in my desk. Every time I open it I think... one small step for Man... one giant leap for mankind. A few billion dollars later N.A.S.A. also gave us Orange flavored - vitamin enriched *TANG!* Go N.A.S.A. go!

> *Have you ever dated someone because you're too lazy*
> *to commit suicide? –Judy Tenuta*

Velcro could be the best illustration of how people are in their relationships today. Couples hook up, or connect, or get together, and it is built on the premise of "We are giving this a try." Now I have chosen to start our foray into great marriage by starting here. Right here. This very thought. I know you could justifiably deny the need to understand this issue, because most of you reading this are already married. So the premise itself seems rather pointless. *Well hey, indulge me for a while.* The information given here I have personally watched change the lives of many people... married people... and single people. In fact this was the only seminar my wife and I did for married or singles for many years. I have taught it as a guest speaker at Metro Bible Studies around the country and together we have shared it with home study groups, youth groups, singles groups, churches, and retreats. My wife and I have used this material on the occasions we have been asked to conduct pre-marital counseling sessions. In our work as an impromptu counselor(s) we have found many people to be married, but not bonded, or at least not bonded properly. Married couple's must understand how their own courtship is still playing a role in their marriage today. Many will need to go back and rediscover some of these principles. Others will have to break some bonds from the past to have a happy and satisfying future with their current beloved mate.

> *I hate that book Men are from Mars, Women are from Venus, because Men aren't from Mars, Men are from Women. Men come out of Women, so if they're screwed up, it's all our fault—stop trying to blame it on other planets.*
> *–Cathryn Michon*

Many of us have gone into courtships hoping to find the right person to *connect* with. The problem with *connecting* is that *connections* can be easily or quickly *disconnected*, whereas with *bonding* - that is not so. *Bonding* is virtually permanent. It is epoxy! *Bonding* is not Velcro, rather… it is concrete! Think about Velcro for a minute. Velcro connects instantly whereas concrete may take days to set, but there is quite a difference in the strength of either bond. Have you noticed that you have never seen a bridge made out of steel that is fastened together with Velcro? *I wonder why!* Most of us have either experienced the joy of bonding or the pain of bonding. Understanding the bonding process will help you create a good bond between you and your spouse (or spouse to be). It will also help you undo the effects of a bad (improper) bond that has brought pain into your life. Do you want simple attachment or do you want to have a "bond" with your spouse? It is a choice of permanence compared to temporary. Read this again if you struggle to understand my wording.

> *Have you ever listened to the sound Velcro makes when it is separated? Ask anyone to describe or mimic to you the sound of Velcro and it will sound as if they are ripping apart a cardboard box. In fact even after Velcro has lost almost all of its gripping ability it still leaves a pretty loud "ripping" sound effect. Velcro relationships rip at the heart of an individual.*

This life-changing bonding information first came to me from a Pastor friend of mine. I had the unique opportunity to sit next to this guy for two years in high school, we have kept in close contact over the years, and then our relationship roles changed somewhat when he became the Pastor at the church where I had previously served in the same position. I have had the privilege of sitting down with this genius of a Man on many occasions and picking his brain on this issue. He helped me get a greater understanding of the information he shared with the congregation and I helped him find ways to insert humorous illustrations. He credits many others with exposing him to this information. Well enough with the personal nods, let us just start!

For Mars Man: The choice to be bonded rather than just connected is an adult choice. A mature choice. It is not going to be the first choice for the adolescent boy. It should be, but it takes a little maturity to recognize the extreme importance of having one person who can truly share life with you in a totally bonded situation. I hope you have the mental aptitude for the challenge. Many of you reading this will find that during your courtship years you didn't have this maturity! That is why you are struggling today. Good news! There is hope. There is restoration. We will get to that a little later. Let us first find out exactly how deeply it has affected us.

For Venus Woman: Most often it is thought that the Man has been the culprit in connecting rather than bonding. I beg to differ my dear Lady. Contemporary media, secular humanistic thinking, poor parenting, and the horrors of abuse has caused many a modern female to become a greater predator than modern Man. The past is in the past... but the past has all to do with your now and your future. May you have the *matzo* to understand the cause and effect that you are coming to live with. May you have the strength and stamina to rebuild that which has been stolen from you.

NOTE: What does it take to have a great marriage? A few months ago a major psychology magazine proposed that question to their readership. It was a simple yet profound question. You can imagine the answers that came in. They ran the gamut from the insane to the mundane. After tabulating all the answers, the *numero uno* response was simply the word *love*. Love! But what is love? I hate it when an answer brings no greater understanding than a question.

1.3

THE INTERPLANETARY DATING GAME

Why are Women wearing perfume that smells like flowers when Men don't like flowers? I've been wearing a great scent—it's called New Car Interior.
—Rita Rudner

You might be surprised to know that there is a universal natural pattern in courtship. This is a pattern set down long ago. This is quite noticeable in the animal kingdom and it seems to be built into some type of natural instinct. These same principles are true in the human populous too. That is to say that there is a correct pattern to courtship, that if followed, guarantees a life-long bond between the two individuals participating in it. I have chosen to explore it extensively in hopes that some of you will discover the missing ingredient in your foundation that has virtually forbidden you from having a great marriage bond.

Be aware that modern society is calling us to have Velcro like relationships, fairly strong, but *dis-connectable* just in case. I believe that God has called us to have eternal bonds that are broken only through the death of that loved one. God designed marriage to be covenant relationship mirroring his covenant with redeemed mankind. There are some interesting verses that comes to us out of Matthew 19:3-6. I want you to read these words of Jesus in both the good old King James Version and the very modern Message Bible.

Have ye not read, that he which made them at the beginning made them male and female, And said, For this cause shall a man leave father and mother, and shall cleave to his wife: and they twain shall be one flesh? Wherefore they are no more twain, but one flesh. What therefore God hath joined together, let not man put asunder. –Matthew 19:4-6 (KJV)

Haven't you read in your Bible that the Creator originally made Man and Woman for each other, male and female? And because of this, a Man leaves father and mother and is firmly bonded to his wife, becoming one flesh - no longer two bodies but one. Because God created this organic union of the two sexes, no one should desecrate his art by cutting them apart.
–Matthew 19:4-6 (MsgB)

These verses are going to be the premise for this chapter. Bottom line, the premise is this: God has called us to the miracle of two becoming one. Now we know that mathematically two does not go into one! You are going to have a lot of one and a lot of two on the floor if you try.

Becoming *one flesh* is something miraculous that God does as we follow his natural plan in our courtship and marriage. Would you like to experience the miracle of two really becoming one? I'll bet you do!

> *I really didn't give Mike a second look when I first met him. He was old. He was a Man - I was a teenager. Five years is a big difference when you are a Junior in High School. But I finally came along. My Dad liked him a lot better than the roller skating referee that I had been gravitating toward. So I gave him a shot. –Terica Williams*

There are four types of love needed to form this miracle bond. Without all of them you are left with a glue that will not set, or a concrete that will never fully dry. *Problems!* With these four types of love given time to gel, a strong and permanent bond can be made. The great news is… that these four types of love develop naturally as we follow the natural courtship steps. It is only when we get outside of the natural steps that we loose the ingredients necessary for a "God" bond. I'm going to give you the four types of love (ingredients) needed for experiencing a great bond in two different ways to help you fully understand the meaning. I will use their Greek words so as to sound intelligent!

> *I never thought puppy love would lead to a dogs life.*
> *–Bob Harrington*

Ingredient #1

Eros

Eros stands as a mysterious magnetic impulse to adore and worship something or someone. It denotes the wonder one feels in the presence of sacred objects. In its purest form it is selfless. It flows from devotion, a desire to create adoration totally free of self-interest and exploitation. *Eros* is most-often the original catalyst, which enhances and empowers a truly great love. *Eros* is that which quickens the heartbeat. *Eros* is most-often that early emotion in a relationship where the heart flutters upon hearing the name of the beloved. *Eros* is the unworthiness one might feel at having that beloved even consider speaking a response to you. One of the holiest and deepest emotions possible to express is the feeling one has when in the presence of a seemingly sacred object of *Eros*. I have often described *Eros* as the emotion one might feel when they are singing songs of worship to the Creator. Let me add that at the very root *Eros* is not physical, but can become physical when acted upon perversely. *Eros* perverted becomes *Pornographic*, but at its core *Eros* is a beautifully awesome part of the bonding experience.

Ingredient #2

Philia

Philia love is often known as "friendship love" because *Philia* takes time to share and understand the other's dreams and passions. It is in the development of *Philia*

that personal dreams and emotions surface and from these come a lifelong basis of
bonded faithfulness. This type of love is developed as two people discover the dreams
and passions and emotions of the beloved at a level in which (non-sexual) secrets are
exposed. It is this type of interaction that allows the honesty needed to become a real
person, and that knowledge is the common thread of *Philia*. *Philia* is further developed
through *lengthy* conversation and mutual non-sexual experience. It could be going
to many a movie and sharing with each other how it moved you and how it touched
your own life story. It can be expressed through the sharing of that inner desire to be
something that life or at minimum your current circumstances have not allowed you to
live out to this point. This is the dominant part of the singles ad that asks for long walks
along the beach. It is mutually enjoyed common interest.

Ingredient #3
Storge

Storge gives the promise of everlasting care. It promises eternal protection. It fulfills
its obligation to its mate to the very end. This is often described as *parental* love or
nursing home love. I saw this in action as my mother spent the last six years of her
life on her back, first at home and then in a nursing home. She had fought a long
hard battle with multiple sclerosis all of her life and now this disease was dealing its
final blows. It took upon the form of Trigeminal Neuralgia, listed as the one of the five
most painful conditions known to Man, and there is little that can be done. I saw this
love demonstrated as my father moved from his home of many years to a little one
bedroom apartment across the street from the nursing home. Every morning he would
dress himself and go across the street to sit by her bedside. It mattered not what time
you came in, there he was, holding her hand, helping her hear the actors on television,
and wiping her tears as he wiped his own. For three years he did this for 15 hours a
day until a stroke landed him in a bed next to her. Until the Sunday afternoon that she
died, my father was by her side. As she took her last breath, this Man who had lost his
ability to speak because of his stroke, took her hand and sang out words he had been
unable to speak, *"Jesus never fails, Jesus never fails, heaven and Earth shall pass
away, but Jesus never fails!"* He then whispered in her ear *"I love you"* and placed a
kiss upon her brow for the last time. This is *Storge* love. It is one of the loves you are
going to have to have to see a permanent bond rather than a temporary connection. It
is the love that allows you to say "For better or worse" and mean it! This is the devel-
opmental period of trust. It isn't built overnight.

Ingredient #4
Agape

Agape is targeted affection. It is "I chose you!" It is "Give me that particular one." For
sake of our understanding, sentiment will be reserved as an adjective used to describe
ingredients #1, #2, and #3. Consider rather that *Agape* represents a calculated
determination to continue in a covenant contractual decision. Wow, that was a heavy
sentence. Let me try to put it another way. *Agape* is a contract, a vow, an irrevocable
promise. *Agape* is determinism and long-suffering personified. Do not freak out
because I claim it has no sentiment. Remember all the sentiment we need is wrapped

up in the first three ingredients. *In the first three is enough sentiment for a million chic flicks... squared.* In this definition *Agape* is the bottom line of the marital contract. *Agape* is often held in contempt by modern culture because it calls for long-term commitment. *Agape* does often cause people to stay together when the *fire* is gone from their relationship. By its very nature, this type of love calls people to continually rebuild all the *other* love types as part of their everlasting promise. I digress... please read on a little further.

Agape is often referred to as God type love, but one quickly sees in the scripture that God type love carries far deeper than *Agape* in many circumstances, but only *Agape* in other biblical illustrations. So if *Agape* is a valid love point for God, who am I to judge? *Agape* is a choice, a choice combined with a covenant determination to carry out that covenant (binding contract) to the ultimate degree. Could *Agape* remain whether the beloved returns the favor or not? I think so. Rather... I know so.

I'm not in a relationship now, but I have a stalker. Which is kind of nice, because at least he calls, and I never have to make plans with him, because he's always there for me. –Pamela Yager

LOVE Making Made Easy to Remember

Allow me to use an acrostic to give you an easy way to grip what should be natural to us had we not been tainted by secular media. It almost seems imbecilic to memorize something that should be the norm. It is like reminding people how to breath. Of course my wife and I practiced that repeatedly in lamaze class, and I'm glad we did or I would have passed out for lack of oxygen. *Babies can suck the air right out of the room, and that is even before the diapers start filling up!* Let us use the letters found in the word *LOVE* to drive home a few points of interest in an expanded way. I will give you four key phrases that may just help this all make sense to those of you who are struggling a little as I often do. *I just read what I just wrote and I don't understand it myself when I say it that way.*

L
LOOK AT THAT!
Representing EROS

Across the room I see something that I really like. She is hot! I like what she is cooking! He is a hunk-o-rama. He is handsome! That guy looks dapper in plaid! *Dat boy is peace out wit da' is out!* I wonder if this beautiful person would even give me the time of day. I'll ask. "Do you have the time... lovely Lady?" *"It is five O'clock... is your watch broke?"* Her response was rather sarcastic... but in *a gorgeous voice. She is obviously trying to cover up her attraction to me!* I adore this person. I could spend the rest of my life looking into those beautiful eyes. Can you see the worship and adoration in these statements? It sounds like the first step in a relationship. A rather *yucky* one from this point of view. Do you understand? My sons first crush was on a Waffle House waitress he said was named *Trainee*.

O
OUR COMMONALITY
Representing PHILIA

Our conversation finds many points of mutual interest. We like the same things. We have similar ideas and values. We both like the music of James Taylor, Jimmy Buffett, Bette Midler, Steven Curtis Chapman, Taylor Hicks, Bill Gaither, Prince, and Sting! We both are English Majors. We both simply adore little Chinese carry-outs. I want to be a missionary... so does she. We both want 2.7 kids! We both believe in living green. She was in the Peace Corps and I was in the Red Cross. We both have a *Go Green* poster in our bedroom. We are both devout Catholic (or Methodist, or Baptist, or A/G, or Amish). We both want to live in Aspen Colorado after we graduate. *We are both unemployed and like it that way. We were both vaccinated as children... how strange is that?* We both like the color purple... but not the movie about it. Can you see how commonality is naturally developing here? Sex is not a good commonality point.

V
VULNERABLY SAFE
Representing STORGE

After spending time with this person you are beginning to see a trust building between you. There is sharing of things you have never told anyone else. Why did you do that? This is a trust building period in a relationship. This is when I expose my inner self to you in a way that you could use to destroy me, but I find that I can trust you. "Touch my face." This is when I allow you to see my weaknesses and expose my heart to you. This is where I see whether you run or stay. This is where we reveal our weaknesses. "I'm Glossaphobic." "I am very insecure about my ability to do my job to the level I'm expected." "I am horrible at the job I do." "I didn't really go to college... it was a trade school." *"I am horrible at speling (yes I spelled that wrong on purpose). If I didn't have spell-check I could never write a book."* "If you lift my hair you can see that my left ear looks like Larry King's nose." "Me too!" "I have to wear suspenders or my belly will push my pants to my knees in a matter of seconds." "I never felt my parents really loved me." "I spent my life trying to live up to the reputation of my oldest brother." "I could only get my cousin to go with me to the Prom." "I have a lot of back hair." "I cheated on my high school English final to graduate." "Don't tell anyone... I have really smelly feet." "I already know... but I love you anyway... I love your stinky feet." "I have a tattoo on my thigh of a pink frog." *"I was once arrested for stalking." "Goodbye!"* Can you see how this time is developing a trust that will have to serve for a lifetime?

E
EVERLASTING COVENANT
Representing AGAPE

This ingredient is demonstrated when we ask each other to be ours for eternity. It is more fully demonstrated when we stand before a minister and a few hundred of our "closest" friends and bare witness before them that we choose to give our deepest love *only* to each other and will continue to choose to love *only* each other for the rest of our lives. It is the signet ring in the royal wax. It is a testimonial to any and all "former relationships" that any questions of choice have now been fully settled! It is a call for the witnesses to encourage us to keep our promise to each other and to them. It is also where we are pronounced Husband and Wife. One of two times we are pronounced anything. Right? Marriage… and death! Please attach no similarities in word definition! "I promise to love, honor, and cherish as long as we both shall live." *But when you die baby… then… then.* Do you see how this holy promise comes into play at this critical time? I am going to include the word *covenant* here. *Covenant!* Holy *covenant.*

> *There is no remedy for love but to love more.*
> *–Henry David Thoreau*

For Mars Man and Venus Woman: When you begin to understand the power of the bond, you will also realize that it cannot be attained unless all the parts of your *love epoxy* is mixed properly and evenly. You need to learn and understand these ingredients as they will become the catalyst for real lifelong bonds. Most all of my marriage counseling (both that which I received and that which I have given) has been a direct response to an improper mix of these ingredients or lack of said same.

The bonding pattern you see noted above is a *natural process* when someone is unspoiled by the world's skewed view of love. Unfortunately we are not of that unskewed world. There is nary a boy or girl on planet Earth that has not been deeply effected by overtly jaded sexual stimuli written and produced by overtly skewed perverts that control our media. *Of course I say that with full respect to both Man, Woman, and the perverts that have skewed us.*

So if that which is written above could be considered a *natural and healthy* bonding process, its very being demands that we attempt to live it out and/or revive it in our own lives for the sake of our own happiness and the happiness of our spouses (or future spouses). Learn them well.

NOTE: You may want to go back and review, or even memorize the definitions of the four types of love before you read the next few paragraphs. If not, you may be scratching your head a little. *That little itch may be telling you something!* You will end up going back and reading it… so go back and at least re-read the acrostic portion of it now.

1.4

COURTSHIP ON A SPACE STATION

Wrongly my mother told me to marry an older Man because he would be mature. Well after twenty years of marriage I have come to realize that Men never mature... I counsel Women to go ahead and find a younger Man!
−Terica Williams

MYTH-BUSTERS

Now I would like to dispel a few myths about these four love types. Some people want to elevate one type of love above the other as if to say that one is *more spiritual* than the other, thus it must be more important. False! Wrong! *Nada!* Every one of these types of love must be present, and present strongly to form a life long bond between two human beings. Some people want to start at *Agape* and end at *Eros* because it seems more spiritual. That rarely happens, and I do mean rarely. I could say never, but there are always rare exceptions. One might also switch the naturally developing order *Eros* and *Philia*. Some would like to start at *Agape* (covenant choice) and end at *Agape* because they think *"total Agape"* is a more spiritual perspective to take. There is a theological/phycological definition for these people and that is "out-of-their-stinking-mind." Some people start with *Eros* and end with *Eros*. This is because something in their past has short changed their ability to go beyond *Eros* and these people quickly become predators. These are the very dangerous ones (male or female) to date, much less wed! Some people have built entire relationships around *Storge* and these people can easily fall prey to enabler or co-dependent mentalities. So we must understand that all of these loves go into the soup that creates a strong everlasting marital bond. Without all four loves you do not have a bond you only have a connection! *Velcro!*

The early State Fairs always had a Tunnel of Love. It should have been called the Tunnel of Lust. It had nothing to do with love. This is a prime example of how our culture has shaped our viewpoint of what love really isn't rather than what it is.

For Mars Man and Venus Woman: You must fight to have all the pieces of your bond. This is the greatest battle of your *pre-marital* life. For those of you who are already married, you are going to have to go back and fix that which is broken. *If you realized you were eating a raw steak you would most likely put it back into the fire to get it cooked properly, right?* If you didn't you might find yourself pretty sick. Your commitment to putting these steps into place in your pre-marital experience will save you months of counseling, thousands of dollars, and years of disappointment in your future married condition. Your decision to go back and learn, and appropriate these in a current marriage will save your marriage. Not only will it save your marriage… it will become for you the foundation of a GREAT marital experience. I'm going to show you how to do that in a few more pages. *You may have noticed that this chapter was very short. I will make it up to you by making the next chapter very long. This way you won't feel cheated. Stay tuned.*

1.5

THREE... TWO... ONE... BLASTOFF!

I hate dating. You look for the right girl, right figure, right face. You search for her. Then, for no apparent reason, your binoculars fog up.
—Mike Builard

I am going to let this chapter be a rambling closure so we can get on to the business of marital life. However you must remember, as I explained in the last chapter's closing remarks, if your love bond has not developed with all four of the ingredients, you are still a little shy of a real quality-bonded love. Now, two or three ingredients can produce a *Post It* note bond, a *Scotch* tape bond, or even a suction cup bond. Sex itself can create a *Velcro* bond. Consider also that if your bonding (love) ingredients (types) are not balanced in amounts, you are going to be out of sync with your bond. Don't freak out! Most people enter into a marriage a little off-center. Nevertheless, we move forward. However, forward motion does not mean that we do not repair a problem. If you were in a boat and discovered it was leaking profusely, you wouldn't ignore the hole. A wise captain starts to repair the leak immediately.

If you look at your relationship right now and find that you are unbalanced in *Eros, Philia, Storge, Agape*… FIX IT! No matter how fast your boat is running, eventually you will take on too much water for your speed to overcome the problem. Take it from a guy who has sunk a real boat before… there will come a day when you are dead in the water and all the bulge pumps in the world will not keep you buoyant. You don't want that on the water or in your marriage.

On a closely related note, let's discuss sex. Did you notice sex is not a listed ingredient in a love bond? Unfortunately for many of our readers, sex has created a false love bond. Sex does create a sexual bond, and often even an emotional bond. But a sexual bond is just that… a sexual bond… it is not love. Sexual bonds are the great deceiver and a great reason why you need to avoid sex until you have all the ingredients of love thoroughly in place. The casual hookup and/or *friends with benefits* world we live in have greatly impeded our ability to achieve bonded love. Don't forget that. Hey, sex is most excellent, but it is not love. People in love have sex. People in heat have sex. Sex is separate from real love. Unfortunately, our media, internet, movies, soaps, and music have told us that *love is sex*, and *sex is love. Nothing rhymes with sex other than hex, vex, T-rex, tex-mex.* So our music has replaced the word sex with love. Don't let a songwriter's lack of rhyming skills and a shortage of a good thesaurus reprogram you. Love is far beyond great to be limited to an exchange of body fluids and a short lived euphoric feeling!

> *Could a greater miracle take place than for us to look through each other's eyes for an instant? –Henry David Thoreau*

Great bonds come with mutual commitment to having all the ingredients in place. Many of you will have to go back to square-one on this. Many relationships have jumped from momentary Eros, to hot-n-sweaty sex, to drive-thru wedding bells in Vegas. There may have been short bouts of Philia or even a church wedding, but only what was necessary to make hot-n-sweaty sex seem legitimate. You may have received some great sex, a new set of dishes, matching towels, and a toaster, but you have not achieved genuine love.

> *Men want Traci Lords in the bedroom, Julia Childs in the kitchen, Lesley Vesser during the game, Cha Cha Muldowney in traffic, Mary Richards at work, Mother Teresa when they come home with leprosy, Gertrude Stein in conversation, the body of Sophia Loren in Boy On A Dolphin combined with the voice of Sade, and to top it all off, the IQ of Anna Nicole Smith, because we don't want to feel threatened. –Dennis Miller*

There is a problem with *Storge*. It is illusive. It is not achieved easily. How do I know that I can trust this other person? I understand. We are in such a sexually supercharged world. There are temptations all around us. There is another problem… porn. Porn gives *Storge* a tough time. Let me put it this way: how can you convince yourself (much more your spouse) that you are singularly faithful to them, if you can't stop chasing the pornography? Does it sound like I am just talking about men? I'm not. There are different types of porn. There is sexual porn and emotional porn. Chasing either ends up the same way… tragic. Men, the truth of your *Storge* will come in your ability to demonstrate it in your restraint on the computer as much as with other women. Women, the truth of your *Storge* will come when you know that you are not getting your emotional fantasy fulfilled watching media, from a man at work, or even a church counsellor.

Here is the problem. Male and female porn is all around us. *It is not like King David's day when you had to own a rooftop to be able to look over the side to spot a woman bathing, then you had to get your guards to bring her to you, and then you had to have her husband killed.* Today it is a mouse click away. Heck, a good Victoria Secret commercial can get you going. What is that all about? I don't believe that Victoria is capable of keeping many secrets.

> *When I hear that someone was rejected by one of the various online dating services I immediately think… wow… they must not have lied on their profile as much as I did. –Rich Praytor*

So this Storge part is going to be tough, I'll give you that. For most of you it will be a one day at a time. Many of you (male and female) have been addicted to either sexual or emotional porn for years. Find a good counselor. Get some accountability. You are not going to achieve the trust factor with your spouse, or even trust yourself, until you do. Enough said.

STOP! Most of you need to go back and develop *Philia*. I hear it often. "We don't talk anymore!" To which the spouse usually says, "I ain't got nothing to say!" You need to work at conversation. You need to work at developing commonality outside of the *Posture-Pedic*. Turn off the stinking TV for a week and start asking questions and listening. Yes, a *television fast is* what most relationships really need. Read a book with a study guide and answer the questions together. I want to speak to my macho brothers right now. No man has strength unless he has strength of expression as well as upper body strength. Don't be half-wimp! True intimacy requires full engagement of the mind and vocabulary. Without communication you are also half-limp! Trust me; you will redevelop your ability to talk when you are pursuing your next spouse, so why not learn it now?

> *Love at first sight is very easy to understand. It is when two people have been looking at each other for years that it becomes a miracle.*
> *–Sam Levinson*

Verbal articulation is perhaps the greatest commonality between *Eros, Phila, Storge,* and *Agape*. Verbal articulation is almost required for any of it to thrive. *Eros* is lived out when the articulation of "Wow, when did you fall from heaven?" is voiced. I know that was cheesy. Deal with it. *Philia* is articulated when we share our dreams, desires, and common interests. And let's be honest… if you can't speak the words "I DO!" you most likely will not get the minister to sign the license no matter how much cash you give him.

But we're married now? Good point. All the more reason to go back and develop that which is needed to make sure it lasts. For the sake of the children, for the sake of your sanity, for the sake of your eternity, for the sake of those who spent an average of slightly over $28,000.00. Go back and develop a bond that will truly bond you. Yes, bond you!

Mars Men: We men talk about things, stuff, problems, and problem solving, especially when we are the problem solver. Women like to talk about how they feel about things. Let me give you a few loaded questions to ask your spouse today. These questions will help advance *Eros, Philia, Storge, and Agape*. Trust me! Try asking the following questions: How was your day? If you could do one part of today over, what would it be and why? What was the worst part of your day? How did that make you feel? What do you think could have happened differently to make it better? You must listen and pay attention. She might question you to make sure you are listening. *Listen as if you care - because you do!* I have just given you the basics of your Doctorate in Psychology in one paragraph. Whereas I believe that good conversation will enhance all of the Love bond ingredients, you must find ways to work on each ingredient's improvement. That is your challenge, men. I believe you can do it.

Venus Women: Your man needs to be the hero of the ball game. He needs to be heard. He wants to tell you about his day, but he struggles with words. He lives in a man's world. There is much grunting, spitting, and sometimes foul language. He is tired and does not know if he has the strength to talk. Help him be what he needs to be and what you need him to be. Be patient. Don't give up. Ask him empowerment questions. Ask him questions that allow him to be the hero, the fixer, the man. Don't ask him how he feels; you decipher that from what he says. Ask him about his day. Ask him to teach you things. Ask him to explain how an engine works, or what the *strong safety's* job is. Ask him questions that allow him to be an authority. Maybe his job beats him up all day. You need to ask him questions that tell him that he is wise, needed, intelligent, and important. When you can do this he will open up to more conversation. That is your challenge, ladies. I know you can do it.

Note: You must commit to enhancing your love bonding ingredients until the day one of you puts their body into the grave. Many of you are reading this book because you know you need help. Go back and work on all the ingredients. Do whatever it takes to kindle and rekindle them all. We are trying to reach the heavens here; duct tape won't do it. You have reached the point where this book really kicks in with great practical living together advice. Congratulations… you made it to part two. *I hope your ready for this.*

2.1

NOW THAT MAN AND WOMAN HAVE GONE TO THE MOON

You better believe Men and Women are different. A Woman will wear thong underwear and complain about her husband wearing his underwear until there is nothing left but an elastic band. This is hypocrisy at its highest degree. I would much rather have two pieces of stout elastic than one lace covered bungee cord.

What do we do now, the honeymoon is over? This latter half of the book is all about living with another planetary being after you have docked the spacecraft. Of course I am talking about… marriage. *Sometimes the space analogies can be a little confusing, but it is a theme and I'm sticking with it.* As you journey into part two, do it with excitement for what "can be" if we really want it bad enough. I hope my single readers will read it too. They might as well get a look into what lay ahead for them and be prepared. Marriage is a journey… enjoy the ride… keep your heat resistant tiles in place… and make sure you have enough fuel to get home.

> *My wife and I took out insurance policies on one another—so now it's just a waiting game. –Bill Dwyer*

Welcome to the twilight zone! Here we are in what seems like an unusual orbit. Not the sweet bye and bye, but the nasty now and now! The real world, and I don't mean the *MTV* reality show about *unreal* life. We are right here and now. You walked down the aisle, made promises you really truly meant at the time, ate the dry cake, danced to the DJ's favorite songs of the 80's, and you find that the *Utopia* you thought you were going to experience is coming up a little shy of the interplanetary vision. Your *Somewhere Over The Rainbow* dream has become a tiny apartment somewhere shy of Tulsa. What do you do now? You've tried clicking your heels together but you can't get back to Kansas. Not that you would want to anyway! *Kansas is a lovely place… I was joking… It's a metaphor… don't write me.* There is hope for you!

> *Women are like apples on trees: the best ones are at the top of the tree. Most Men don't want to reach for the good ones because they are afraid of falling and getting hurt. Instead, they just get the rotten apples from the ground that aren't as good, but easy. So the apples at the top think something is wrong with them, when in reality, they're amazing. They just have to wait for the right*

Man to come along - the one who's brave enough to climb all the way to the top of the tree. On the other hand... Men are like a fine wine. They start out as grapes, and it's up to Women to stomp the crap out of them until they turn into something acceptable to have dinner with. –Marie Lynch

Part Two of this book is about the now. Without understanding the first half of the book you would have been doomed to go on dreaming and unfortunately waking up to a disappointing reality. OUCH! *That was harsh... wasn't it?* The reason I included the first half of this book into *this book* is because foundations are important. Jesus said, "No Man builds a house without first counting the cost." I think he meant to say, "No *intelligent Man* or Woman builds a house without first counting the cost, finding a good contractor you think you can trust, and still getting it all in writing." You may disagree with me, but consider first His saying, "Wise people build their houses on the rock... and foolish people build on sand." YES... *that was a slight paraphrase!* I feel safe in standing before God with that statement.

I was watching HGTV the other day in my hotel room. I love those home makeover shows. I am not happy with the number of emasculated men (notice I did not capitalize *men* this time) who dominate the decorating scene, but at least they aren't pushing it on me like they do on the networks. This particular home renovation I was watching went bad, and went bad quick. The basement that was being redone, caused the original foundation to collapse. That collapse caused cracks in the walls and ceiling of every room. Rooms that were originally nice and strong and beautiful and well decorated, now looked like the Rolling Stones had used it for a hotel room... and it was a great party! The show went through a number of contractors in their attempt to fix it. They eventually chose to jack up the house and pour a new foundation. So with much fear and trepidation they began the arduous task. I believe it was six months later that they were now back to square one, and able to begin work on the basement. Now [all] the other rooms in the house can be started on. When a foundation is shabby it will *effect* and *affect* every other room in the house *eventually*. *Eventually* takes time... but *eventually* always comes.

The responsibility of marriage goes on long after the vows are said. I might even venture to say that is where it really gets tough. This is where the quest is no longer there for a Man. The hunter has hunted and come home with a quarry. This is where the expectations of the bride kicks in. All that the bride imagined is now coming to pass or passing before her eyes. It can be a grueling time if both parties are not as interested now as they were on the day before the wedding.

Many of you reading this book, if not every married person should go back and make sure they have a good foundation going into this process of making a great marriage. For some of you it will take the starting of a dating process all over again. "But we have children, we have houses, we have cars, we have mortgages," you say. So do I! I understand that you are where you are right now. Sometimes you simply must to go back to the beginning and start again. So I whole heartedly suggest that you who have found cracks in your foundation by the examination of it... get out the jacks and start jacking. Spend your time in "REPAIRING THE SPACECRAFT" before you go much further. In fact if you repair the spacecraft correctly, you might not even need the rest of this book. I wish I had been privy to this information before I entered the marriage arena. I wish I had been privy to all of this information before I started dating. If so, it might not have taken twenty-three years to get to this point in my own marriage.

This is very important

For Both Planets: It is going to require something of everyone if these space stations are going to function interdependently. Union is mutual work. It cannot be one-sided, although it may have to start out that way. A great marriage is also going to require you to be a person of humility. *Pluto has to admit he aint really a planet. Sorry, no great space analogy here.* Humility, I believe is the one trait that most allows us to achieve success in any circumstance. Humility allows us to see our own faults and thus change, and thus become better. The meek shall inherit the earth, and also inherit great marriages. If you embark on this journey into truly becoming one in body, soul, and spirit with your spouse, you are a brave individual. You are the quality of person who deserves to have a great marriage.

2.2

REPROGRAMMING ANOTHER PLANET

How many Men does it take to change a lightbulb? Who knows... Men don't change! –Kelly Sisney

Apparently both the Venus Women and Mars Men are working to re-program the other to be more like their own self. The Women are trying to make Men acceptable at a five star restaurant and the Men are trying to turn the Women into *Nascar lovin' independently wealthy Hooters waitresses* who are also real good with kids! Since we have started trying to change each other there has been a few setbacks. This rebellious Man has fought to remain the wild Lion! Man has fought to retain his position as king of the food chain and not succumb to these feministic tendencies toward frilly, fancy, and shiny. Woman has raised the whip and the chair in an attempt to tame the lion! For years Woman has continued to stand her ground in an effort to retain some microscopic semblance of civility in this male dominated frontier.

Women love Men with problems. We look at a Men the way an HGTV looks at a old building. "How can I remodel this one?" –Donna East

The truth is we really don't want to change each other too much. If Men became all that Women dreamed them to be, sensitive, warm, caring, and nurturing... they would have a lesbian on their hands. Real Men are not going to be everything a Woman is... and also a Lion! Not gonna' happen! Nevertheless, there can definitely be some improvement in the male actions. Just because the Man is the king of the jungle doesn't mean he has to poop in the living room! He can be trained to go outside or at least on the newspaper.

Where have all the caring sensitive Men gone? Well they've already got boy-friends. –Kristy Byers

Now on the other side of the street, Men need to learn to appreciate that which set Women apart from the start. Our "Macho" is contingent upon their being a damsel in distress. No damsel - no distress - no macho needed! Women would do well to remember that too. Let us males remember every day that we do not want to be married to a testosterone-less us! Their femininity is of great attraction to us. It should be! Certainly they can be helped to understand our psyche, but we do not want them to be Men. That would be one sloppy house and the toilet paper would never get changed!

> *Love is blind—that's why we will always have*
> *more hippopotamuses. –David P. Dean*

I mentioned this in the introductory chapter, but I want to expound on it a little more in this chapter. Gunther Gebel Williams the famous lion trainer said "You can train a lion, but you can never tame one." Ancient text has an obscure passage that depending on the version you read from, talks of the Woman's task with Man being that of training/taming a wild lion or wild animal! Well Training can be done, but it is not easy. Really Ladies, you love a Man for the LION/ANIMAL in us and have often held in contempt those Men who we have seen reduced to domestic house cats. *Pay close attention to my wording here.*

Training is done by a reward system. The animal does this task - he gets a reward. The key is to find a reward that the lion will like, something that you know they will respond to. Some of the Men are smiling and some of the Women are cringing thinking about this. *Some Men are panting thinking about taking out the trash as they read this… hoping you their spouse is up to this chapter.* Men are born traders. For centuries of our history we hunter-gatherers took what we had and swapped it for what we wanted (or needed). *It has only been in the last few centuries that we have not hunted or gathered something to trade to get one of you… a female! We are not that many generations from trading seven sheep, two chickens, and a barely used Yak in exchange with your father for you… and your sister!* You may think this *contemporary trading* (I prefer to call it positive reinforcement) concept is ludicrous… but it works. Many Men are brilliant, and many are barely a few I.Q. points above a potty-trained furry carnivore. It does not matter. Either way, do not whip the puppy or the lion! The puppy will chew up your shoes and pee on your rug. The lion will bite you and it hurts! You cannot beat the lion into submission. You cannot insult, browbeat, or guilt a lion into becoming a teddy bear. It will never happen. You can only help/teach him to respond in a more positive way. Those who try to use intimidation techniques will soon find out that they are getting the opposite effect of what they are desiring.

> *I wish they would make those dog-shocker collars for Men. And every Woman*
> *in this room knows why! –Kristy Byers*

In working this training one must always keep in mind that we Men might be taught to dress up, brush our teeth, and even wear deodorant… but at some point we are going to roar if for nothing more that to express our macho image as King of the Garden! We will bark to show others we are here. Women, in general would do well to understand that they have made great strides with Men in just getting us to occasionally comb our miens and wash between our toes! So if you set off to train your lion… be aware it won't happen overnight, and clear your head of the idea that you will ever tame one completely. *This is why some old Men sitting there at the mall mumble.* They may have had all the fight beat out of them, but there is still a little lion left in their soul, and it's going to talk back. Unless bred in total captivity, Men will be Men, at best ruthless, maniacal, insecure, boisterous, egotistical, messy, sloppy, and lover of things done in dirt. It is our nature to return to the dirt from where we were created. Rejoice in the differences we have and celebrate the miracle of a union between two so unlikely a pair. I have already stated this in the introduction, but I am told that most of you didn't read that.

I like a Woman with a good head on her shoulders. I hate necks.
–Steve Martin

Now I might mention that contemporary Women have come along way from their centuries old female counterparts. *The 1970's circa Virginia Slims commercials taught us that!* For the sake of my point, let me compare Women to lovely domesticated house cats. The lovely and *most recently* domesticated kittens are enjoying their new found comforts, complete with indoor kitchens and baths. There has certainly been domestication and change in the female world as well as in the male world. *I have yet to meet a Woman who in this present age would rather be cooking over an open fire pit… the iguana… her husband clubbed earlier in the day… in the back of the cave… near her favorite sleeping rock.* Yes our Ladies have come a long way from the 1800's, much more the 800's.

I know quite a bit about the domestic house cat. Years ago I owned one that would hide in the basement and drop down out of the ceiling and stick her claws in my head for no apparent reason other than she (the cat) obviously found it amusing. Again let me reiterate that I'm talking about a cat, not a wife here. *Although I have to admit that has always been a secret fantasy of mine*. A cat appears to always be calm and collected… BUT… when you surprise them… BOOM! *"Rampart General… we have a pulse… boy do we have a pulse!"* Some Men would do well to think of their female counterpart like a cat. If you want to get them motivated you need to surprise them. This is extremely hard to do considering they don't miss much (cats or Women). Little surprise gifts of kindness or affection, no matter how little, as long as it is unsolicited, brings great reward. That is all I will say for now. *Dare we talk about this again? Probably not.*

Had Adam not sinned… we would all still be naked… there would be no seasonal wardrobes… and no fashion scene… and no Shopping Malls! That makes me believe that [certain] groups have actually had their lives enriched by others mistakes.

For Mars Men: You married a domesticated, complicated, hopefully regenerated, sophisticated, gentle, respectable human of the female kind. She is different from you in many ways although she at times seems quite the same. Enjoy the differences and relish in the adventure of it all. Where there is no quarry there is no longer a hunt and no longer excitement and no longer adventure. We thrive on adventure. Relish in the excitement of each days adventure. You married Eve… she is different from you…

this is why you didn't marry Steve. Difference is good... very good! I know you are the *King of the Jungle*, but you *aint* in the jungle anymore, this aint even the zoo, and this precious female has a lot to teach you. Yes, teach you. You need to learn the stuff too! You don't know it all. Do the rest of the male population a favor and become teachable. Humility is a greater sign of strength and wisdom than arrogance was or could be. Unless you do, you are going to make the rest of us look like moronic barbarians by association. *Help the brothers out here.*

For Venus Woman: You have married a domesticated, complicated, hopefully regenerated, sophisticated, rough, tough, respectable human of the male kind. *You expected me to bash on the Men here... didn't you? Well I will not.* You married exactly what you wanted and found out that you have linked with a lifelong challenge. Your challenge is taming (training) him without breaking him, or you, or both of you. Make sure in your desire to domesticate him to your level of culture, that you do not *train out of him* everything that made him exciting to you in the first place. I have seen that happen a few times. *It isn't pretty! It is rather pitiful.* Let's remember that their are things this guy can teach you too, and you need to learn them. Be teachable.

> **Humility is a greater sign of strength and wisdom**
> **than arrogance ever was or could be.**

For Both Planets: Now I want to drop in a very related issue at this point. I addressed it briefly in a paragraph to singles earlier, but now I want to expound a little more to my married friends. Attaining a great marriage can be achieved if both parties have a teachable attitude. Without a teachable attitude there is little that can be done in the merging of our different worlds. *I know - I know... that you may be right about everything and there is little anyone can tell you because you are all-knowing, all-right, and all-brilliant.* I'm honored that you would even read this book. You probably should have written it. Sorry, that was too sarcastic. Being unteachable is what the Bible clearly defines as a fool! A lot of people marry them. They shouldn't have... but they did. So let's ask ourselves a few questions. Can you look back on your life and identify some major mistakes that you have made? Have you ever been solely responsible for a big mess up? Not things that *[would have been]* successful if somebody *other than you* hadn't gotten involved... I'm talking about the situations where "you" have made stupid mistakes. Well? Yes or no? Can you list at least ten? How about twenty? A thousand? *I could fill a book with my own personal failures! It would have to be a multi-volume set!* If you have found yourself to be, or to have been an unteachable person... repent. Repent now. *Get down on your knees and ask God to forgive you for being perfect!* If you have found yourself married to an unteachable fool... pray. Pray hard. Pray real hard. Ask God for someone to come along that your spouse will respect enough to learn from. Until that happens you will have to work on you alone. *So on a good note, it's not like you will be bored during the wait.*

2.3

TWO PLANETS - TWO ORBITAL PATHS - TWO THOUGHT PATTERNS

Love often intoxicates; marriage always sobers.

It was interesting in my study of Planets that it said of Venus, "It may be the least hospitable place for life in the solar system." I have no idea how scientists who have never actually been to this place could attach such a negative connotation to this planet. *Some of you sarcastic Men may be saying, "That sounds about correct!"* Now let me say right here, "Shut up and be nice!" On the other hand, the good old internet provides a lot of useful Mars information. Apparently the Viking landers performed experiments to determine the existence of life on Mars. The results were somewhat ambiguous, but many scientists now believe that they have no convincing evidence for life on Mars. Optimists point out that more experiments will be needed! *Some of you Ladies will use this analogy to say, "If there is no life then there is no brain activity."* Thus proving Men are brain dead! Ladies, Lighten up a few minutes! *We can all make fresh nooses or a shank in our craft class later.* Both Men and Women need to quit searching for ways to find fault with each other and work together to find the commonality of our species and our individual likenesses.

Can't we all just get along? –Rodney King

While searching for a good illustration for the differences in the brains of Men and Women I found myself sitting down to eat at a Women's prayer luncheon. *No I was not in drag… I was a guest speaker… but I do own a kilt.* The tables were decorated very nicely, the napkins were folded, there was silverware at every place setting. How different this is from the guys weekend at the lake. We too had a large hall to eat in, but it was rather simple. If you wanted a napkin, pull one from the paper towel rack. That was until our lack of planning quickly revealed that we did not bring enough paper towels and had to cut up an old sleeping bag. If you wanted silverware (which is definitely an option at the Men's event), grab for yourself a plastic fork or use your Swiss Army knife! Even the food was different! While the Women enjoyed a delightful chicken salad containing a mixture of chicken, mayonnaise, sliced grapes, raisins, and celery, lightly salted on a bed of lettuce, the Men enjoyed BBQ chicken and slightly burned beans! The beans were fresh from a can! Of course there was lots of BBQ sauce! It is a rule at a Mens event. *Anything is palatable if it is covered in enough good BBQ sauce.* Pretty much that was it. Yes, I forgot, we also had a few potato chips, but it was pretty much chicken, beans, and chips… for lunch and dinner… both days!

Eve was a jealous type… I heard that she used to count Adam's ribs every night to make sure he hadn't been seeing other Women.

Now one could argue that throughout the day both sexes ate some of the same type of meat. The Men had some grapes for a snack in the fishing boat, and there was a bag of raisins I saw in somebody's tent. Men certainly didn't mix them together as if to create a single entity! We could handle food best if the edible items were kept separate. Like a kid who didn't want the peas and carrots to touch, we were now demonstrating a more mature illustration of what it means to be single minded. Now I am *not* talking in particular about the Biblical model for single-mindedness, but rather the way our minds process things is *one thing* at a time. My wife has often commented that I have a one-track mind… It was not meant to be a compliment when she said it! Nevertheless there is some mysterious truth to our single or one track style of thinking.

Think about crayons. Man are the 8-pack… basic colors… no frills. This 8-pack contains every color a man could possibly use… and a few extra. Women are like the 96-pack with a sharpener. To a Woman this 96-pack contains a very small sampling of a few colors she might like to use… and even with all these choices they will need to find something a little more plumbish Red to match the towels in the bathroom.
–Gordon Douglas

Men are single minded! Men can barely walk and chew gum at the same time. Women are infinitely minded! Women can walk, chew gum, talk on the phone, look at their Day Planner, correct the kids, change a diaper, and drive a mini-van at the same time! Mind you that they are not driving well according to a male standard… but they are driving! Sorry. That comment was so sexist it should be removed from this book… and I am going to talk to the publisher about it too! *I am appalled that I even wrote that.*

Why can't Helen Keller drive? Because she's a Woman. –Dave Nowak

This single-mindedness comes in very handy to us in the business world. Men thrive in business because they can go to work and lose themselves in their work. Whatever was happening at home can be placed in another file, the (home or personal life) *escape* button has been clicked! Women have everything connected… all the time… 24/7… 365 days a year. Women cannot leave home and forget about what is happening today at school with their youngest child. Men can go to work and forget they even have a child! This is why statistically Men reach higher levels in the workplace. I know you feminist will give me a few other reasons that will involve the phrase "Boys Club," but please argue with the statisticians not the scribe.

Women will never be referees at pro football games. They would be throwing flags for things committed in the previous quarter… just because they happen to remember them. –Rich Praytor

Women are always thinking, always remembering, always connecting. Men are frequently on the border of having their entire body go into suspended animation. My wife thinks I have an *escape* button on my butt. I often set it off by just sitting down in a chair! Are you aware that Men have the ability to virtually shut down their brain? This should explain a lot of things to you wonderful ladies out their! *Hey you can't fault a computer that isn't even plugged in, right?* Or maybe I should be more exacting and explain that Men's *brains* have the ability to virtually shut off. Stop! Suspend operation. *I'm talking about that little spinning color wheel on your Macbook… when it just keeps on spinning… and spinning… and spinning!* Scientists have studied the brain waves of Men and discovered that males can virtually stop all mental activity! *Flat line. No measurable electrical impulses. Beeeeeeeeeeeeeeeeeeeeeeeep! "Rampart General… we have no pulse… we are starting an I.V. with D5W and Ringers Lactate… do you copy?"* It is a marvel to science that Men can reach a point where their brain is so completely inactive… and yet they continue to breathe! *One Woman blurted out at one of our seminars, "But when they do resume normal operation, they are probably thinking about sex!"*

Inside my head is a Lava Lamp struggling hard not to get out.
–Bradley Bean

These same scientists (made up of both Men and Women) found that Women in a fully relaxed state are still connecting neurons, thinking, preparing, planning, and creating scenarios. Women have no *ESCAPE* button! The brain of a Woman connects continuously and with every thing else in her brain. This is why my wife and I can be arguing about an illegal left turn I made on the hi-way and before you know it she has connected my driving to my underwear being on the floor, the time I forgot her birthday in 1991, the fact that I never did fix the ceiling fan in our last house before we sold it, and how my mother fits into this picture even though she has been deceased for years! WOW! A Woman's mind has a billion little wires and they are all connected! Everything is connected! *They are the poster children for multi-tasking!* The whole time she is connecting all this stuff I have reduced my thinking to, "Uh… I wonder what time the game is coming on. Maybe I should catch a quick snooze."

I love to sleep. Sometimes I daydream about taking a nap.
–Thor Ramsey

Many Men live to shut down the mainframe whenever possible! *This is why we like fishing. Who cares if we catch fish. We don't even like fish.* We desire nothing more than to hit the *ESCAPE* button and go to our mental Lava Lamp. We all have one and we just want to go there… please let us go! Going to this place of *male nirvana* is a goal of Men. Some of you Women have the audacity to want us to explain it to you or even get you a membership… but we can't! The club has been chartered for Men only. If you were there it would be too noisy! There would be too many questions to answer, you would want to see all the rooms and redecorate, and then our *ESCAPE* button would have become a full system scan disc and re-boot! That isn't [escape] in our world! It would be installing *Windows Vista* in our perfectly satisfying DOS world.

So where does that leave us?

For Mars Men: Understand that for your spouse everything is related to everything else. I mean EVERYTHING! Breakfast is related to lunch which is related to supper which is related to the price of groceries which is related to the children which is related to a church which is related to the book she read last night and the movie you saw together two years ago when you were on vacation which is somehow now related to your treatment of her MOTHER. You must make every attempt to connect all the dots if you are going to see the same picture that she does. It is very detailed. You have a television... some of you may even have picture in picture! This female operates from the control chair of a television broadcast studio. There are a fifty monitors out there and each one of them has picture in picture... and TEVO!

For Venus Women: You must remember that Men are like victims of a pre-Alzheimer's syndrome. Very little is connected, or even remembered from yesterday, much less from three years ago. Deal with Men as soon as there is a problem because in two hours he will not remember what even happened much less remember what he said. *I am convinced that male politicians are not liars, just really forgetful.* Thus they chose to create scenarios that they wish would have happened, and might have happened, could have happened, should have happened, but they really can't remember what actually happened. *It could have been a band... it could have been sniper fire. Who knows?* Well I guess that last line was not a very strong case study for Men... but you get the point.

For Both Planets: If we think differently it would make sense that we would need to keep that in mind when we are communicating with each other. You would not call Botswana and expect them to understand you in English. Well maybe we American's would... but it is not right... and down deep we all know it. When will we give our spouse the same consideration that we do another country? "They should have learned our language by now," you say. Maybe they could say the same thing. Ever been to Miami? New York? Things are different from town to town and thus obviously from planet to planet. What we think is right - isn't always what is. *Get over it.* Welcome to the real universe. Welcome to Diverse City!

2.4

INTERPLANETARY COMMUNICATION

No wonder my wife lost her mind; she's been giving me a piece of it every day for 20 years. –Nazareth

Wouldn't it be a good guess to think that if two completely different cultures came together, that there might be a slight language barrier too? Oh they may use the same words, but it doesn't always mean the same thing. It's kind of like *SYNONYMS*. When a Man says "Frank" he means a hotdog and a Woman is thinking about honest communication. When a Man says "Fidelity" he is referring to the frequency response of his car stereo speakers. When a Man says "We should get married" he means that someday… sometime… in a few years… you and he should fly to Vegas and make it legal. When a Woman hears the "M" word, she is thinking that she needs to immediately call the printer with the date to print on the invitations she has already picked out months ago. On the other hand, when a Woman says "I want honesty" she means that she wants the whole truth - and nothing but the truth. Conversely, when a Woman says, "Be honest, do these jeans make my butt look big?," she is actually wanting to be reassured that she looks thin and awesome! Every Man knows that or at least will find it out within a few days of marital bliss.

> *I told my Mom that the teacher gave us synonyms…*
> *and she told me not to eat to many because it would*
> *spoil my supper. –Jackson Bailey*

We have fifty different variations on the Bible just trying to keep the understanding of words up to date. How much more would language play a role in our personal differences? If you know Latin American Spanish, I dare say that you could understand someone from Spain, but maybe you shouldn't try to interpret a life altering legal document for them. There would be some interpretive and cultural differences. I had a friend who was trying to greet a South American village in what he thought was their dialect. He spoke what he thought to be, "We greet you and bring you welcome from the United States of America," His words In their language, though very close were, "We greet you and then bring you all to the United States of America." *This guy went from missionary to slave trader in a few mixed up syllables.* It was a matter of miscommunication. Sometimes we misspeak other times we are just misunderstood. All of us do.

When deaf people talk to themselves... do they move their hands in front of a mirror. –Leland Klassen

Our communication skills are very different. How this happened I do not know. Technically we all grew up in the same neighborhoods, with the same parents. Many of us had a sibling of the opposite sex living in the room next to ours. There should be a greater understanding by this point in our cultural development. Unfortunately there is not! *Apparently the theory of Evolution does not extend to language.* Watch little children in pre-school. The little girls will sit and talk for hours... they don't even need someone there to talk with. They will talk into the air. Like an incessant sugar-charged gerbil their little mouths will articulate stories and songs. On the other hand little boys will grunt, snort, gurgle, punch, slap, and hit. There is seemingly very little intelligent thought going into their communication. Don't they get better? Not much! Does not the watching of John Madden on Monday Night Football prove this theory? Have you ever heard him go into one of those mindless word chatters that say absolutely nothing? Madden might say, *"The thing about great football is that it has got to be great foot-ball or it just isn't great football... and these guys are playing great football. I have been to games where they didn't play great football and great football wasn't played, but this is great football and it doesn't take a rocket scientist to know what great foot-ball is and isn't."* Many of the females reading this book are scratching their head right now and trying to figure out what that John Madden statement was really trying to say. Another demographic (mostly males) are saying, "That's right... you tell em' John!" This same group is also wishing they had thought of something as profound as that to say. *Of course many of these Men have consumed a very large pitcher of beer during the game.*

If you can't say something nice, say something that could at least be inter-preted to be nice if you looked at it a certain way.

The experts say that Women speak an average about 30,000 words per day. That is the average! My wife can top 40k before noon if her cell phone is fully charged! *I do not know who got the job of sitting there with a handheld counter.* Men have about 12,000 words a day. Some would say they have about 12 words. Men come home from work having used up most of their word quotient for the day. If I have to spend any time on the phone, my words are on overdraft by 4 O'clock! I know that some of you don't believe me. You read my books and say, "Anyone who can use that many words... he can talk." You would be mistaken. I can type a lot of words... I can talk for about an hour before I am ready for a break. I struggle with just being tired of talking. *I have to confess that I have pretended my phone was going dead just because I was tired of talking on the phone. Have you ever done that? Certainly not to my wife... but to other people.*

Men come home from work with 12 words left to speak. What's for dinner? Where's the remote? And are we fooling around tonight? And those are all in the form of a question! –Gordon Douglas

Not only do Men run out of words, but I believe we also run out of the ability to hear and comprehend words. I can speak 12,000 words a day and intake about 25,000 words a day, after that I am milk-toast! Some wives want to go back to their rooms after our seminar sessions and start to talk about everything they learned. Be careful. Your Man may be over his word quota for the day. This will only lead to you thinking he doesn't care. So ask him first! *This is no truer than you thinking because he can't seem to digest a ninth helping of your cake that he doesn't like it… NO! He is just full of your great cake!*

I have come to believe that Mike and I really do speak two different languages. There are many similar words… but they mean completely different things. Sometimes I wonder if his language even has twenty-six letters. Are grunts considered words? –Terica Williams

So you will know… in general, Women are way too descriptive for Men! Again, In general as a Man, I don't care what somebody was wearing and how much of a good deal they paid for it when you tell me about their most recent car accident. I don't care who the other parties involved are related to, or how many kids they have and their approximate ages and school grades, or whether they were wearing those cute little capri pants they got on sale at *Wal-Mart* last week. Just tell me, "Are they Okay?" and if they are, "Where's the remote?" I care about the people but I am not moved or motivated by what they were wearing. You may include the condition of the car for interest sake… but only briefly if was a notable classic!

I've heard that a dog is a Man's best friend. That explains where they get their hygiene tips. –Kelly Maguire

On my way in here today I clipped a little add from the Delta Airplane magazine. Headlines read "A MUST SEE FILM." It is for the movie *Atonement*. I hate to mention that because I do not know if it is a good movie or bad movie at this point. They didn't give a rating. So understand that I am not endorsing it in any way. Don't write me. I just want to point out the quote they used to describe the movie. It is delivered from actress Keira Knightley, as she says about the movie, "It's a story that isn't about what is said, it's about what isn't said. You learn what you are saying and then what you are meaning." Wow… that must be deep… because I didn't quite understand that statement at all. Do my *fellow Men* out there understand that? *I don't either.* I'll bet our ladies do… even though they don't get *"Great Football is great football…"* This is how it has been for Mars Man and Venus Lady… give or take a few exceptions throughout history. So in an effort to bridge the language gap I submit the following suggestions to you both. This alone may solve half of your post-marital conflicts.

For Mars Men: First off, take your time. Communication with your beloved is not intended to sound like the introduction of a top 40 radio song. Slow down. Talk to your beloved. Be as descriptive as you possibly can. She is a delicate being who pictures things in 4-D and needs the colors and textures to get a feeling of what is happening as much as simply hearing what was said. Make sure she understands the words you are using in her dialect. She is as concerned about the *feelings* involved as she is about the *facts*.

For Venus Women: Just as you need to see the picture with great depth of field, your beloved will overload his sensory perception with too much information. Share with him in as little detail as possible. He doesn't care who anybody in the story is currently dating or who they are related to. He wants to hear what happened. He cares little for the color, hair style, or brand of clothing anyone in the story was wearing. Bonus information only clouds the main concept and will cause him to nod off into la-la land. *Lengthy descriptions are like aerosol valium.* So you must pick whether you are giving him the facts, the description, or the feelings. Don't deliver them all simultaneously. *That could cause the computer to lock up and all the 8 crayons to melt right in their little yellow box.*

2.5

MARS INSULTS WHILE
VENUS EXHORTS -OR AT LEAST TRIES

Terica believes my criticism would be better received if I sandwiched the critiques between two compliments. So I turned to her and said, "You have two beautiful earrings... between them... is the densest brain I know!" I don't think she had that in mind.

From the time they are little, boys spend their lives cutting each other down. Their group interaction consists of hurling insults at each other in an effort, if even half hearted at best, to declare themselves to be the greatest lion of the herd and the *super-est* of the supermen. On the other hand, little girls grow up complimenting each other. "How I love those shoes!" "Where did you get that beautiful dress?" "Those earrings go perfectly with that necklace." You can see it in adulthood as Women seek even to get inanimate objects to... as they call it... "compliment" each other. Little girls are told how lovely they are and boys are told to be tough. Girls are truly sugar and spice and everything nice. I have two of them... I know. I greet my oldest one with "Hello my beautiful little princess." To which she responds, "Daddy... I'm a very big princess." *I'm sure in a few years she will not be as quick to insert the word [big] into her princess ideas.* Every day I tell my daughter how beautiful she is and how much I love her. I tell my boys to go take a bath because they smell like rabid monkeys! *They laugh.* They love smelling like monkeys. They are proud of the stench! Stench is a badge of honor for a boy. It means they have played hard and can prove it. *Last week my son was bragging about getting his first arm pit hair! That is so male.* This variance in basic upbringing accounts for the reason Women desire to be "adored" by there spouse. It has been bread into them. I'm not saying it is bad, just that Men need to realize it is an axiom, the same way the *lion* is bred into us!

> *Honey, I think your jeans have shrunk again... I don't mean that in a bad way... I mean that jeans are not made the way they were when we were dating... No... that is not what I meant either... I think I need to just stop talking and go to sleep on the couch.*

In light of this marked adolescent difference you have a stage that is now set for some pretty tough verbiage and heavy misunderstanding in later years. How many of you Men have spent the afternoon looking for a picture frame with the perfect shade of *southwestern shrimp* and *penne teal* to compliment the floral arrangement on the dinning room table? Point proven! *How many of you Ladies have ever complimented your Lady friends on the rankness of a bodacious after dinner belch, or something even worse?* Point proven again. Now certainly I'm sure there are exceptions to that observation… maybe some of you do… *you go girl…* but give me the benefit of the doubt and a little levity for a few moments to prove this point.

> ***Mike's major language is sarcasm. Even when he is being kind it comes off with an air of crassness which I find very distasteful. But returning sarcasm for sarcasm never helps the situation. I know that now.***
> ***–Terica Williams***

Now I am sarcastic! I know it. I have a series of books that seem to glorify sarcasm as a spiritual gift. My mode of communication is sarcasm, and people pay me big money, at least what I consider to be big money, to express that sarcasm openly in large crowds. So now Mike (me) comes home to Terica (my wife), who has been exhorting and giving and complimenting all week and starts in with his sarcasm and coarseness and backhanded insults. No matter how little he means of it… it is going to cause emotional unrest to come to the *Little Miss Compliment*. I know that there are different love languages because I saw a book on that subject at the bookstore. In fact I even wrote a terrible little parody of them after I was given a "LOVE LANGUAGES" poster. It came anonymously. The handwriting on the poster tube looked vaguely familiar! It listed *Words of Affirmation*, and I do love to be told how great I am. So affirm away. Second was *Receiving Gifts!* Count me in… I have a few great ideas for you to bless me with. Or just give me a gift certificate to Bass Pro Shops and we'll call it even. Coming in third was *Quality Time. Hey, two out of three is not too bad.* I was always one who felt that a great gift (a new vacuum cleaner) could more than make up for quality time. An upwardly mobile Father has taught many a son that axiom. Fourth in the good Reverends list was *Acts of Service*. Little things done by the other person to tell them you care. Now my list of possible acts that are called service might tend to be rather different that my spouses. *I tend to think that my going to work every day is an act of service.* Now coming in at number five is *Physical Touch*. Hey, I'm into that! If you got the time… I am ready. Let's touch!

> ***I wish you could hold down a job the way you***
> ***hold down a Lazy-Boy!***

A comedian friend of mine Gordon Douglas (whom I quote rather often) does a show entitled *Things I Wish I Knew Before I Said I Do*. In this hilarious presentation he expresses how Women need seven non-sexual touches a day to feel loved by their spouse. He says when he does this there is always some guy who will reach over and give his wife seven little taps. "one, two, three, four, five…" Then he looks at her as if to say, "Now you know… what I like?" That is not what is meant by these touches. Since Gordon told me this, I have been actively seeking ways to wrap my arms around my wife and give her meaningful squeezes to let her know I care. This has been with good result! Women want and need to be held and adored. Whether they admit it or not, Men want to be held and looked up to as well. They need to believe that you really believe their Superman cape is really real.

Consider this

We must overcome our inability to combine our individuality into mutual compatibility despite the fact that we have the language barrier! It would behoove us to invent a electronic pocket translator today. Now since there are no male to female or female to male electronic pocket translators currently available, let me offer some suggestions as we close this chapter.

For Mars Man: First off... cut the sarcasm. Save it for the office and your football buddies. Build your wife up by letting her know how special she is. *And she is!* She married you. Let's be honest, you did good. It is surprising to me that she gave you a second date. Yes, I heard about that *first date* fiasco! *I read the blogs.* Honor her for being her. Honor her for the place she has as the mother of your children. Remind her often that she is still a priceless Princess in your eyes. Let her know by your words, though they may be few, that you still want her and need her in your life.

For Venus Woman: Lighten up. Your Man lives in a world of upwardly mobile cut throats who claw, scrounge, and insult their way through the day. If the average Man began to exhort his peers they would think of him as *effeminate*. He is coming home to a different time zone and a different language. Give him some time to remember where his ship has landed. Nicely help him remember he is at home and not on the basketball court or in the sales office. Remember to tell him how much his masculinity means to you and the family. Make him feel as if he is a great lion.

2.6

MARS GRAVITY - VENUS GRAVITY

Mike would allow me to give him a back rub every night of our lives if I would do it. He would probably never think that I would like one myself every now and then. He would chalk it up to what he would call my motherly instinct. Well this [mother] doesn't give back rubs every night! That came as a complete shock to him. I don't mean that in a bad way.
—Terica Williams

Mars Men are takers and Venus Women are givers. Men like to take in and Women like to give out. You can give to a Man and they will take. You can give more and they will take more. They will build barns and sheds to hold all the stuff that you will give them. Women are givers by nature. It starts with the simple verbiage that was listed in the last chapter and has continued throughout the rest of their lives. With few exceptions it is the Women who do most of the giving around the home. The family organization… family schedule… family feeding… family clothing… usually done by the Women. They give to you, the kids, church, social events, neighbors kids, and the list could go on and on. If schedules are going to be kept and children to be at school on time it will be because the Woman gave of her time to do it… most of the time. *Left alone I don't know if the kids would eat until at least ten at night… and then it would be hotdogs or microwave dinners.* As I stated earlier, there are some exceptions, even great exceptions to the typical that will be used in this book, but I am talking in a generalization here. Women do take also… but in a different way. We will get to that… be patient.

When I met Mr. Right I had no idea that his first name was Always.
—Rita Rudner

I remember the first time Terica looked at me and said, "I have been giving and giving and giving and giving and I don't know how much more I have to give!" That blew me away. I had no idea! I was dumbfounded. The truth of it was that she did like doing that stuff, but she conversely needed to get her needs met to have the strength to keep being the giver that she wanted to be for me. I need to fit in the word *reciprocal* here somewhere.

If a Man finds a wife he has found a good thing – but if a Man finds a million dollars in small unmarked bills it would be better if keeps quiet about it.

Now again, to keep my male readers in check, it would behoove me to mention again that Women can be great takers too. I have yet to give a gift to my wife only to hear her say, "This is too much and you just give me too much." This is quite possibly because my gifts are so few and far in between that they do not seem as extravagant as they possibly could. I have friends that have dedicated their lives to be extravagant givers to their wives, and I have watched their wives accept their new position of *taker* without flinching. In fact they have become rather skilled at receiving.

Think about it this way...

The key is learning how to take from each other. I hate trinkets! Women seem to love them. I see no reason to own more than one watch. I have three pair of shoes to my name. One pair (my brown SAS loafers) I have had since we were married over twenty years ago. I can afford new ones, but that would be rather wasteful, especially when that money could be used for something important like missionary work or a new Ping Titanium Driver or a new Bowtech Guardian archery bow! So *giving* for me is best received in small doses, but with a substantial and useful gift. To me a gift needs to be *useful*... if it is to be considered great.

This Man (me) can hardly stand to buy flowers because they just wilt and are thrown away. I would rather wait and "save up" for a year and buy her something really nice. My wife seems to prefer many little gifts throughout the year. A nice romantic card, a little note, a bag of the new jumbo M&M's, a non-stale Chic-O-Stick, a new hair-clip, diamond earrings, or really anything shiny! That "shiny" statement sounded negative... I apologize. *Deal Ladies... deal.*

I imagine Venus Woman might learn how to take from a Man in a way that would allow her to feel as if he is giving. Without a doubt it would advance both of our worlds if we understood the mindset behind the gifts that we gave each other. I have heard it said, "It is the thought that counts." Wait a minute! Is that the way we really want it. If that is true then we should all be satisfied with just *thinking* about each other. It is time we stood up as Men and Women and began to meet the needs we were each born with, or at least give it our best efforts.

What is the definition of a tragedy? Marrying a man for the money and finding out he has no money.

If you want to be a great spouse you need to understand what your spouse really wants. The Woman wants and needs to be loved and adored. It comes from those early Princess days. She needs to be reminded of her inner beauty and her outer beauty. Men need tools in which to fulfill their role as hunter/gatherer/builder/protector/super-hero/golf pro. I have mentioned this many times in other books (please take a short break and buy them too). I have bought for my wife gifts that would have been best bought for Men. I once purchased a new vacuum for her birthday. OUCH! You don't buy a Woman a vacuum for a birthday present. I know that now. Boy do I know that now!

At the time I thought the vacuum was very insensitive. Ironically I just had my forty-first birthday and I found myself asking for a new Dyson vacuum and being excited about the possibility of getting one. How things change with the years. –Terica Williams

For Mars Men: Your spouse needs adoration and appreciation. She needs to be told through your words and gifts that you adore her and think about her often. She needs to feel as though she is a pearl of great price. She needs to not be defrauded. What? Defrauded? During your courtship period we showered her with adoration, value, and words of worth. Where did that go? Were we lying? No… certainly not. We were (along with honesty) using our cunning-crafty hunting skills to secure the quarry. We were in the throes of *Eros*. Get back to that time every day. It is now time for us to use our cunning-crafty hunting skills to keep the quarry happy and satisfied. Adoration and compliments are like vitamins to a Woman. Hugs are a B-12 shot. Little gifts are relationship steroids. *Love notes are female Viagra!*

For Venus Woman: Your spouse needs adoration and appreciation. He needs to be told through your words and gifts that you adore him. He needs to feel as though he is a pearl of great price. He needs to receive from you the respect your actions promised him in the courtship period. He needs to be shown (not just in front of the children) that you appreciate his leadership and authority as the one responsible for the family before God.

For Both Planets: Do not defraud your spouse no matter how badly you feel your spouse is treating you. Returning wrong for wrong is never right. C'mon, you teach your children this… live it! There was a day that you stood and promised to "love, honor, and cherish" each other… stand by your word. Now in doing this you must constantly keep in mind that you both demonstrate your love for each other and to each other from different perspectives. Attempt to see your spouses gifts as coming from where they are coming, a good, but different planetary heart. A Man may buy his spouse a vacuum cleaner with the total misguided belief that this will be a great way to tell her of his adoration and heartfelt love for you. Be wise enough to understand his motive, and softly, at a future time help him to see what really motivates you. A Woman may look at what she does all day in keeping the house clean, tending to the children, working a job, as a showing of affirmation to her love for her spouse… but it most likely will not be received that way. A Man expects the same thing from his work. We all have ability to consider what "we do" to be the great work, and what "they do" to be merely what ought to be done. It is time we get over it and get on with merging our planets.

I think what we all need is a good dose of old fashioned repentance. In this case that would be saying to God, our spouse, and ourselves that we have been missing the mark in both giving properly to each other and in how we interpreted the gifts we have been given from our spouse. If we have been keeping our generosity at bay, we need to let it loose to tell the other how much they are appreciated, adored, respected, and loved. When will you do it? Today or tomorrow? Well tomorrow rarely becomes today. Don't be stingy here. Be extravagant.

2.7

THE HEALTHY MARS / VENUS DIET

Married Men live longer than single Men... but married Men are also more willing to die!

Let me let you in on a little secret. Married Men do live longer than single Men. I said this one time at our seminar and a Man from the back shouted, "But married Men are more willing to die!" That is sad if it is true in his case, but it does not have to be. Married Men and Women enjoy better health than single people. Statistics show that they make more money despite the fact that the tax codes unfairly tax them. Married people have better sex! Yes... better sex!

> *I don't have a girlfriend. But I do know a Woman who'd be mad at me for saying that. –Mitch Hedberg*

My good friends *Jay and Laura Lafoon* have a wonderful marriage retreat that takes place all across the country. It is called *Celebrate Your Marriage!* You should go to it sometime. I have had the opportunity to entertain at these events a few times across the country. It is a weekend of *partying* over the fact that you have each other. It always takes place at a very posh romantic looking resort overlooking the ocean or lake, which makes the Ladies happy, and there is always a golf course nearby to keep the Men excited about being there. *Conversely... our last seminar took place at a lovely Motel 6 just out side of Tulsa! I must say they had a delightful Continental Breakfast included!* The entire *Celebrate Your Marriage* weekend sets the mood for some awesome intimate personal time together as couples truly come together in celebration of their marriage. Did I mention that there are no children at the conference? There is a cause for celebration right there! I often jokingly refer to their weekend retreat as the *Consummate Your Marriage* Weekend. To which Laura always gives me an obligatory giggle though she actually finds it a little rude, and Jay gives me a "You better believe it buddy" wink. *I know that wink my friends! Yes... I know that wink.*

We Need To Celebrate Our Marriage!

The media has systematically crucified marriage as if it were a horrible thing. They have been on a witch hunt for the institution of marriage since the days of *Sodom.* Surf the channels and you will find people complaining about their marriage and glorifying their illicit affairs. Well... why do people want to get married then? Even those who are in illicit affairs end up with a desire to eventually marry. Why is that? Well life just works better when you are married. As I stated in the first paragraph of this chapter... Married people have a better life and of course the part about the better sex. That is right. Clinical studies have shown that married people have better sex. This stems from their freedom from inhibitions, comfort ability, and general familiarity to express their own self without the need to perform. It comes from their freedom to *not* be perfect. The freedom to be naked without holding in their gut! The freedom to not be able to last for four hours... as the commercial seems to promise. Sex for show is not the best sex in the world. *I would much rather enjoy driving a race car than be filmed having fun driving a race car.* I had much better illustrations than the one used, but that was the only one I could find that did not seem crass. So please make no correlation with the race car to anything else.

I explained to Mike that holding in his gut while he weighs himself does not make him weigh any less. I found out that he was not trying to weigh less... He was simply just trying to see the numbers. –Terica Williams

Medical studies have declared that for a Man, being single, is equivalent to smoking two and a half packs of cigarettes a day! Maybe? I don't know. I have never personally done a comparison. I would have compared the single life to wearing bug spray with 90% *DEET* or *huffing Sterno. Now with those I have done comparison tests!* Wow... two and a half packs of cigs... a day... *90% DEET... Sterno...* dang... married life is good for you. It is good for a Man, it is good for a Woman. We need to celebrate the institution of marriage. We should all shout, "Hip-hip hooray, hip-hip hooray for marriage!" I might make my seventieth birthday because of this Woman. She brings to my table something that cannot be achieved in a single world. I bring to her table something that she needs. I don't know that we will ever quantify what vitamin it is, or exactly why, but none the less married people are healthier, happier, and again of course there is the better sex issue to boot.

It's Not Just An Apple A Day That Keeps The Doctor Away

I purchased a book a few years ago after David Letterman had his near death experience. It was co-authored by one of the Doctors that performed his heart operation. At least I think it was him. The good Doctor was certainly somehow involved. The book is titled *The Owners Manual.* It is a *complete guide* to being healthy. *There were lots of big words in it too.* One of the statements that stuck out to me as a Man (I don't know if the Ladies will gravitate to this bit of knowledge like I did) was a little tidbit of information about cancer rates. it said that a Man who reached orgasm twenty-one times a month had a more than 50% reduction in certain types of cancer. I don't know if that is true, but I would certainly consider volunteering for that study group. I think every Man in America might join me. When it comes to our health - we can't be too carful. I will talk about sex a little more in a forthcoming chapter. So let's drop the subject for now with the simple understanding that we... Men and Women are good for each other. We compliment each others shortcomings and stabilize each others abuses. Though we

want to be individually whole people, marriage brings a larger than 1+1=2 complete-
ness to our lives.

So how do we respond?

We need to stop looking at each other as the "Old ball and chain" or the "Old Man"
or the "Old Woman." Let us celebrate the amazing miraculous joy of marriage. Let
us celebrate what it does for us and to us and not what [in our apathy] we have let it
become.

For Mars Man: Choose today to look again at your spouse with the same fervor and
desire that you had when you walked down the aisle. Refer to her as your Princess,
treat her that way, and require your children (and/or step children) to do the same. She
is your queen. Place her ahead of the guys at the office and the boys you play poker
with on Tuesday night. They are not making you healthy… left alone they would do
nothing but make you sick. Or dead!

For Venus Woman: Choose to see your husband as the King of castle. Look at
him again as the knight in shining armor that rescued the damsel in distress (let me
symbolize for a minute) from the dragon of singleness, singles groups, singles bars,
or whatever! Require your children (again both types) to respect him as the king of the
castle. This Man is bringing, can bring, will bring fullness and adventure to your life if
you will let him.

For Both Planets: Go to your corners and come out celebrating. Every week place
a cake on the table with candles and sing "Happy Marriage" to yourself… complete
with the corny harmony on the end. Let your children see this celebration. Good times
or bad times celebrate what is good for you. Celebrate what is good about your marriage. In this celebration you will find more joy, and increased reason to celebrate.
Parties begat parties. And by all means… work to keep that cancer rate at bay
(wink-wink).

2.8

MARTIAN MONEY - VENUS MONEY

The difference between Men and Women can be reduced to this; Women don't find farts amusing! –Justin Fennell

When I go to the Dominican Republic I always make a stop at one of these little currency exchange banks in the Miami airport. These are the ones that look like a little VW Bus from the 60's only smaller. You need these if you are going to a foreign country and want to buy anything you might need, like food. *So you know that I'm going to stop!* My U.S. money is not acceptable in the Dominican Republic. One dollar is worth one dollar to me, but to them it is rather worthless. *To be honest it is getting that way here in America... the dollar just aint worth what it used to be.* If I want to work in the Dominican I am going to have to use their monetary system, or at least understand the exchange rates to thrive in the foreign country I am going to. This chapter has to do with the way Men and Women value each others contribution to their marriage. In fact you might say that we have different coinage and a very different exchange rate!

Every Woman needs a Man... Because there are some things that go wrong that you just can't blame on the government, the kids, or bad luck.

Let me put some illustrative thought to my rather proven hypothesis. We (Men and Women) place a preconceived value on everything we do. We subconsciency say my time is worth... [this] much. We feel that certain actions we do have an intrinsic value to the family... and to our spouse. Both sexes do this. They may not be keeping a paper ledger, but you can be sure that somewhere in the 10% of the brain a Man uses and the 90% a Woman uses, there are at least a few neurons keeping track. I know that Men and Women place different values on their roles within a marriage. Let me speak for the Men first. I get up at 2:30 in the morning (yes that is for real) and head to work (usually at least a five hour commute with two plane changes) and get to my event on time, I sleep for a few hours and head to the next event. My mind says that I have just deposited $2500 into my relationship (with my spouse and family) bank. Now when I get home from the airport, I do it without stopping off at the music store and my mind says, "BINGO... there is another $500 investment in my relationship to my wife.

I'm a *greeeee-aaaat* husband and father." Once I got home, before anybody, including myself, ate too much food I led the family in a combination prayer and devotion for thirty seconds... $100! I sit down and watch ESPN television with the family, and maybe even a *docudrama* or two and I am headed to the bedroom a wealthy Man. I've got thirty-one-hundred dead presidents in my account for my work, sweat, and toil to spend as I please. *Not to mention the money I earned last night but came to bed too late to spend it.* That should buy me a back massage and maybe even a little extra attention... if you know what I mean!

A lot of people wonder how you know if you're really in love. Just ask yourself this one question: "Would I mind being destroyed financially by this person?"
–Ronnie Shakes

Now I understand of course that my beloved Venus Woman got up early too, but she got to stay at home with the kids, so that really kind of evens out because she likes to do that. Right? She always wanted more kids! More kids - more time with kids - same thing? She is blessed! She took care of the house and cleaned the clothes, but this is really her dream house not mine. I would have continued to live happily in the twenty-eight foot Airstream Camper at the Lazy Dayz' Trailer Park had it not been for her. I guess I will give her a few bucks for doing the laundry, let's make it $10. Now she does home school our oldest son, but in actuality I pay taxes for schools so home schooling is just a choice that she made, so I shouldn't really be expected to pay extra, but I will give her $10 as a show of good faith and mutual respect. *I'm a giver!* She did make a good meal for me and I do love her chicken and rice. It is pretty tasty, but really the dinner is a wash because she had to cook for the kids anyway and I paid for the meat in the first place. I will tip her according to the 15% rule of food value based on myself being the only legitimate paying customer. I will give her $2, I did have to get my own drink refill! She sat down and watched television with me for a few minutes and did refill my drink once or twice, but one trip she was already coming bringing me microwave popcorn, so it was not like it was a special trip. Okay I will add a $1 if you insist! She is going to finish the night with a strong $23 in her account. I will let her find a way to balance that out with my effort for the day... I'm sure she will see the difference and offer extreme appreciation... if you know what I mean.

It is hard being human. Look at the prototypes, Adam and Eve. That's a lot of pressure, being the first people. You make one mistake, every-body hears about it. You're constantly answering embarrassing questions about how you messed up. "Okay, for the five millionth time... I was sitting around, minding my own business, and she offers me a bite."
–Brad Stine

Now let's look at the female perspective for a minute. The female does not even work in the dollar system. She works on the point system. It does not even convert to the dollar system. *There is no mini-bus in the Miami airport that can even exchange on this level.* It would be like trying to convert the metric system to a musical note... ouch! This lovely lady has been up half the night keeping baby quiet so I could sleep and still gets up at 6 in the morning. For that she takes for herself a point. She multi tasks

cleaning, washing, shampooing, driving, arranging, scheduling, and refereeing fights
for eighteen waking hours and for that she allows herself ten points. This precious
Jewel of the Nile makes supper from scratch with a little help from Betty Crocker all
the while balancing one child on her knee with the three others clinging to her heels,
all the while doing some Sunday School preparation, and for that she takes five
points... but not any points for the Sunday School stuff, that is for the Lord. She serves
the family during dinner, this includes the feeding of the baby from her own spoon
while she tries to eat something and clean up a spill from the two year old, and for that
she will humbly take another point. She joins her husband watching Monday Night
Football and makes his popcorn and delivers a few soft drinks thinking this will acquire
her three more points. She bathes the kids and gets their bed clothes on in time to get
to bed before he nods off to sleep watching *Leno* or *Letterman* and thinks this ought to
round me up to a total of about 25 points. She is headed into the quiet part of the night
with a good point score! Not to mention the points that she has been accruing over
the last twenty years of their marriage. This kind of point spread should earn her a few
minutes of good honest communication with her spouse and a few minutes of simply
being held by something other than a drooling two year old. *When you look at it this
way, who could fault her?*

> **My friends tell me that I have an intimacy problem.**
> **But they don't really know me. –Gary Shandling**

Now this beautiful Woman fully understands that her Mars Man got up early too, but
work is a joy to a Mars Man. Isn't it the *Males* way of escaping the troubles and trials
of daily life? So there will be no points given to him. Mars Man worked long hours,
but Mars Man was the one who chose to follow this career path instead of going to
work for her father at the brokerage firm... plus I got to enjoy hours of commuting and
listening to sports on my new XM satellite handheld receiver! No points! Mars Man
did come straight home without stopping off to spend time with the guys and that was
good, but that is what he was supposed to do, but Venus Woman will give him a point
to demonstrate her compassion. I only get one point because she knows I wanted to
stop but felt guilty about it since that sermon series by Pastor Smith and the Promise
Keepers rally I went to. Now I did pretend to be interested when she (though unsolicited) began to tell me about her day, and I got another point. Later I did not answer
her when she was asking me questions about my day during the replay of the Top Ten
plays of the week... I lost a point! *This is not fair because I didn't hear her talking.*
I do find a way to pry myself out of the Lazyboy recliner and actually brush my teeth
before coming to bed, and I get a point for effort. *Woops... I farted under the covers
as I got into bed... I loose a point.* She is going to total my points (in that secret tabu-
lation room hidden deep in the cortex of a Woman's mind) and I could finish the night
with a few points, maybe? *If I do not continue with the flatulence.* The spouse says
to herself, "I will give him a chance to make it up to me by spending some quality time
with me in the few minutes before we rush off to sleep. This will be a way to balance
that out his effort with my effort for the day... I'm sure he will see the inequitable difference and offer extreme appreciation and give me a few minutes of quality adult

conversation." By that she means conversation that does not involve talk of Barney or the Power Rangers.

Add this up on your calculator Mr. Banker.

We have a problem here. If we continue to try and balance an emotional two-person checkbook with different forms of money we will end up overdrawn and bitter. Yes BITTER! We are going to have to lay aside our attempts to balance out our service and serve each other as Christ served the church. The Bible clearly demonstrates how we are to esteem others.

Let us each esteem each other more highly than we do ourselves. –Phil 2:3

Now that verse demonstrates a *tough* love. Nevertheless it is the degree of love we have been called to give. If we continue to try and trade favor for favor, eye for eye, and tooth for tooth, we will end up favor-less, eye-less, and tooth-less. *Tooth for tooth is is one of those southern biblical phrases. Had it been a yankee phrase it would have read teeth for teeth!* Pardon the humor there, but I think you get the picture. Do you?

For Mars Man: Stop thinking of yourself as the only giver in the family. You are one of two givers… and receivers. Your job is not to see what you can get in exchange for what you do, but rather how much you can give… and give… and give.

For Venus Woman: Stop thinking of yourself as the only giver in the family. You are one of two givers… and receivers. Your job is not to see what you can get in exchange for what you do, but rather how much you can give… and give… and give.

For Both Planets: Those of you who actually read both responses saw a striking similarity didn't you? I hope so. It was meant to be such. Do you get it? I know you may think this is inequality at this point in your marriage. It may be. Your job is to serve correctly no matter what the return is. You tell your children, "two wrongs don't make a right." Well live with that as a standard of integrity in your own life and marriage. If anyone deserves our best it is our spouse. Be the best giver you can be.

How do you say "I Value your contribution to our Marriage" to your spouse? When was the last time you said those words? Why don't you make an attempt to say it every day for the next 30 days and see if your world does not change for the better… for you and for your spouse.

2.9

GREAT SEX ON EITHER PLANET

We survey people about their private sex lives, and write manuals based on data gained by watching people perform sex in a laboratory setting. To junior high students we teach details of sexuality forbidden to previous generations. At the same time, I know of no greater failure among Christians than in presenting a persuasive approach to sexuality. Outside the church, people think of God as the great spoilsport of human sexuality, not its inventor.
–Philip Yancey

Ouch! Mr. Yancey tends to go right for the jugular vein! Billy Graham says about Philip Yancey, "There is no writer in the evangelical world that I admire and appreciate more." So if Dr. Graham likes him… so do I. Am I going to talk about sex in this book? You better believe it. In fact, I may even throw in some pictures or at least line drawings to keep your attention! *Quit thumbing to the next page! I was joking.* Some of you gave questionable rise to that statement already. Well good! By the time you have reached this chapter you should be a little weary in your reading marathon. Sex is important. It is a reciprocal mysterious additional part of a magical bond set up by God himself (see part one of this book). I am also going to talk about it because I like sex! I like it better than football, baseball, or basketball. Give me a choice of a golf game or having sex and I will take the latter. *In fact… do both! It will make the back nine be much more exciting!*

Having twins is like ordering the buy one-get one free Vacuum Cleaner special on the Home Shopping Network, it seemed like a good thing to do at 2 a.m. and then nine months later UPS truck pulls up, you sign a form, and then he pulls your purchase through the Mail slot on the front door. If that isn't bad enough… three days later your husband is checking out the Home Shopping Network again for another great deal. –Kim Mauldin

Sex has been important to mankind for a long time. Adam's introduction to Eve was, "Be fruitful and multiply…" Adam found out exactly what *a pleasure* designed by God could feel like. *He also discovered the meaning of the phrase, "Tomorrow Adam, I've got a headache!"* Certain parts of a Man carry great importance to him. When God decided to get the attention of the Men of Israel, consider where he went cutting first! Ouch! How would you have liked to be at that college initiation? Now you thought the hazing at your college sorority was tough! I would not want to be associated with *PHI*

BETA SNIPIT in any way shape or shorter form! I don't care if I get a free t-shirt and the opportunity to join Skull & Bones! Count me out.

My wife's body is brighter and more fascinating than a flower, shier than any animal, and more breathtaking than a thousand sunsets. To me her body is the most awesome thing in creation. Trying to look at her, just trying to take in her wild, glorious beauty, I catch a glimpse of what it means that Men and Women have been made in the image of God.
–Mike Mason

All through the Old Testament God continued to get Men's attention in this rather obscure place. I believe he did it because he knew that he had made mankind to deeply treasure that particular area of their body. No other organ could bring him so much pleasure. For years God judged the *true and the brave* by asking them to go chopping in a pleasure filled area of the most sensitive organ in the human body.

Women often criticize Men for the fact that clinical studies have revealed that Men think about [sex] every thirty-four seconds. Other clinical studies have also declared that every Ninety-one seconds a Woman thinks about [murdering] someone or being murdered... Lighten up ladies, really, get off your hypocritical pony, put down the gun, and come over here and cuddle!

Does Man have an infatuation with sex? *Duh! Like you didn't notice.* Man is born with a distinct longing and attraction to the female body. Even without the information given to him by high school sexual educational instructors has somehow figured out exactly how to make it all fit together. Little boys wonder about it, middle school boys dream about it, big boys enjoy it, and aging boys try to find chemicals to keep enjoying it. Don't tell me sex is not a big thing... it is. Viagra and the chemical equivalents of it is a billion dollar business. Television ads are certainly selling more dollars worth of little pills than they are Bibles.

Although sex has been a big thing for mankind for many years, it does not seem to be as big a thing for Women. Personally I think that is because of the selfish way in which Man has treated Women in regards to sex. *That is just my honest opinion.* Maybe had Man treated Women with the same goal of mutual fulfillment from the beginning, Women would be more apt to be as desiring of it as we. Just my opinion, I have no scientific data or century old polls to refer back to on this one. Now I know that it is a huge overstatement, to say that Men are always more interested in sex than Women. *That is like saying every boy dancer in the musical Cats has a lisp, they don't!* There are some wives who have a greater desire for sex than their husband. *These Men are often despised by other Men and should not mention this as a problem in a group breakout session for fear of being beaten back to his senses!*

Women today expect too much from Men. They want a heart of gold... a card of platinum... and buns of steel. Unfortunately I had feet of clay... hair of gray... and abs of buffet. They want Prince Charming! I was like the Prince formerly known as charming. They want a knight in shining armor! What's wrong with a knight with a shining forehead and a belly as a round table. –Paul Aldrich

My wife is a wonderful Lady with a great sense of humor. She is my meter of funny when I need a little help on a joke or two. She is the editor of the bits and skits you hear in my shows and on the podcast. She gets it! There is one type of comedian that really bugs her. One type that she can't stand. It is the female comedians who base there entire show on how Men are nothing more than horny monkeys and how Women spend their lifetimes trying to figure out ways to deny them any sexual satisfaction. She has no compassion or place for that type of humor. She says, and I quote, "I'm sick of female comedians parading around the premise that Women don't like sex. We do like sex. Many of us like it as much or more than the Men do. Quit stereotyping Women!" *Now there's a great Woman for you my friends… and she is all mine!*

What a great truth. Women do like sex. God created it to be mutually pleasurable to say the least. It has been Mankind's debasing of sex, and abuse of sex, and the racing into sex, and the cheapening of sex, that has taken some Women to a place where the joy of sex has all but gone. If you treat sex as an act to receive release of your stress and sexual tensions and testosterone overload, you have reduced sex to that horny monkey status. However, if you view sex as the mutually rewarding culmination of *Eros, Philia, Storge, and Agape,* then you have a beautiful icing on a four layer cake of love. I'll bet if both parties started treating sex as a holy act before God, instead of a "git'r-done" transaction, your sex life would improve… in fact it would become mutually attractive.

There is a church in the town next to mine who has placed billboards all over town with an interesting challenge on each sign. Some have touted this to be nothing more than an advertising ploy to reach super-sexual Man and get him into the church. I don't know… and I don't care. They are challenging every married couple to engage in sex every day for thirty days. They are challenging every non-married couple to abstain for thirty days. I will not deal with that part. I believe my views on that point are also well expressed in the first part of this book. Yes… thirty days of sex. Every Man I know likes the idea. I'm not sure if all the wives do. In watching the interviews I have seen every wife lay claim to having great joy in it as they chose to participate. Now this challenge was not to have sex for sex sake. It was a challenge to experience intimacy that culminated in the sexual union of two healthy-whole-hearty lovers. I can't wait to try it. I have not been home for more than about five nights at any one time for the past fifteen years. *But this challenge is on my bucket list!* Maybe you should make it a part of yours. What could it hurt? I believe if married couples would participate in sex more often, Men might not be as apt or even able to rush to the finish line each time. As they aged - they couldn't. *If you know what I mean.* If we shared this intimacy more often we might see a little more work in preparation arena and not just in the grand finale. *Again… if you know what I mean.*

> **Oh the joy of finding a Woman who works out everyday and oh the agony of finding out that she can beat you up. –Paul Aldrich**

There are keys to having great sex. Just like there are keys to making a great cake. I can't help but notice I choose to use a food illustration to parallel sex, but it is another of my favorite distractions. The key to great sex, in fact having sex at all is that it is not designed to be started and finished in two minutes! People always laugh when I say that in the seminar. It is true. According to my internet research (so it has to be true), those scientists who have dedicated their lives to watching people have sex, those Peeping Toms cloaked in the guise of white lab coat, have given us an average. They say that male sexual experience averages two minutes in length! Two minutes! That is an average. That means if you include some of these "If you have an erection that last for more than four hours call your Doctor" Viagra jockeys, you have a large group of people who are not making it to two minutes. Is it any wonder Women aren't feeling like there is anything in this for them?

Before marriage, a Man will lie awake all night thinking about something you said; after marriage, he'll fall asleep before you finish saying it.
–Helen Rowland

Gordon Douglas told me about a friend of his that does a talk entitled Sex Begins At Breakfast. Now don't worry, I believe he does this as part of a marriage seminar. I specifically did not mention the speakers name in case he was speaking at your child's youth camp this summer you would not freak out! Gordon told me this speaker postulates that what you do the first hour of the day will determine the outcome of the last hour of the day. *Or for some of you selfish guys, what you do the first two minutes of the day… will effect the last two minutes.* Again, I haven't been to his seminar, but I imagine that this great author of multiple books understood that foreplay is not saying, "Hey baby wanna' dance?" If you want incredible sex you must have the *foreplay* (which is not a bad word) begin hours before you go to the bedroom. Foreplay is part of the entire sexual experience. It is not something you "have" to do, rather it is a something you "get" to do. Celebrate it. *Foreplay* starts with communication.

Now I was raised in a very Baptist home. Conservative Baptist! *With a capital C!* I'm sure there are family members rolling over in their graves if they can see me type this much less hear me talk about it. *Growing up we never talked about sex… it could lead to dancing!* Unfortunately I'm serious when I say that. The *Birds & Bee's talk* I got from my dad went like this; "Son… aaaaah… aaaah… you know Men and Women are different… aaaaah… and there is going to be times when your wife is going to… well… let's talk about this later." That was the first and last conversation my Dad ever had with me about sex. *For the record I have since figured it out!* It took twenty plus years of marriage and a few kids before I came to the point where I feel that I have a decent understanding of the general process. I do like to keep in practice. *Isn't there a Bible verse that talks about using your gifts or they will be taken away? I certainly don't want that to happen.* I remember sneaking over and reading the *Song of Solomon* during a boring sermon when I was a High School student. Wow! *Don't let Mom see you reading that or you could be put on restrictions from reading the Bible.* There is like some *heavy petting* going on in that book. My Pastor never preached out of that book. In a Bible class I took once the instructor told us it was a secular illustration about the love of Christ for the Church. That is dead-wrong! Let me take you on a little journey into this book if you don't mind. I do this purely so that we understand that God is not opposed to sex. You may have been somehow taught that. *Wrong!* He invented it! Certainly many parallels can be given to our own sexual experiences, and also the church (if it had bosoms), but this book is about real people having real foreplay and real sex.

Now let us set up the book for just a moment. Written by Solomon the son of David. For your interest this is the son of the union between Bathsheba and David. Before you closet theologians judge this too harshly please remember that this is the son who would carry on the blood line of the Messiah. If you ask me, Solomon seems to be somewhat of a *Don Juan* when you begin to read his words. In fact, I am a word crafter, but I stand fully impressed at this Dude's ability to throw down on a phrase. It sure beats the *roses are red* stuff I have written throughout my dating years.

Solomon writes…
Dear, dear friend and lover,
you're as beautiful as Tirzah, city of delights,
Lovely as Jerusalem, city of dreams,
the ravishing visions of my ecstasy.
Your beauty is too much for me-I'm in over my head.
I'm not used to this! I can't take it in.
Your hair flows and shimmers
like a flock of goats in the distance
streaming down a hillside in the sunshine.
Your smile is generous
and full-expressive and strong and clean.
Your veiled cheeks are soft and radiant.
There's no one like her on earth,
never has been, never will be.
She's a woman beyond compare.
My dove is perfection,
Pure and innocent as the day she was born,
and cradled in joy by her mother.
Everyone who came by to see her
exclaimed and admired her
All the fathers and mothers,
the neighbors and friends,
blessed and praised her:
"Has anyone ever seen anything like this
dawn-fresh, moon-lovely, sun-radiant,
ravishing as the night sky with its galaxies of stars?"
One day I went strolling through the orchard,
looking for signs of spring,
Looking for buds about to burst into flower,
anticipating readiness, ripeness.
Before I knew it my heart was raptured,
carried away by lofty thoughts!
Dance, dance, dear Shulammite, Angel-Princess!
Dance, and we'll feast our eyes on your grace!
Everyone wants to see the Shulammite dance
her victory dances of love and peace.

Shapely and graceful your sandaled feet,
and queenly your movement-
Your limbs are lithe and elegant,
the work of a master artist.
Your body is a chalice,
wine-filled.
Your skin is silken and tawny
like a field of wheat touched by the breeze.
Your breasts are like fawns,
twins of a gazelle.
Your neck is carved ivory, curved and slender.
Your eyes are wells of light, deep with mystery.
Quintessentially feminine!
Your profile turns all heads,
commanding attention.
The feelings I get when I see the high mountain ranges
Stirrings of desire,
longings for the heights
Remind me of you,
and I'm spoiled for anyone else!
Your beauty, within and
without, is absolute,
dear lover, close companion.
You are tall and supple, like the palm tree,
and your full breasts are like sweet clusters of dates.
I say, "I'm going to climb that palm tree!
I'm going to caress its fruit!"
Oh yes! Your breasts
will be clusters of sweet fruit to me,
Your breath clean and cool like fresh mint,
your tongue and lips like the best wine.
Yes, and yours are, too-my love's kisses
flow from his lips to mine.
I am my lover's.
I'm all he wants.
I'm all the world to him!
Come, dear lover-
let's tramp through the countryside.
Let's sleep at some wayside inn,
then rise early and listen to bird-song.
Let's look for wildflowers in bloom,
blackberry bushes blossoming white,
Fruit trees festooned
with cascading flowers.

And there I'll give myself to you,
my love to your love!
Love-apples drench us with fragrance,
fertility surrounds, suffuses us,
Fruits fresh and preserved
that I've kept and saved
just for you, my love.

Song of Solomon 6:4-7:13 (Message)

If you think that is *over the top* you should read it in the King James Version. *OUCH... you might need to take a cold shower.* Here is a Man that knew how to talk to a Woman. Here is a Man who had obviously saved up enough words to whisper these to his lover. Instead of using all of his words grunting around the water cooler about a third string quarterback in a fantasy camel racing league, this guy was jotting a few notes in his *Daytimer.* A pretty good trade if you ask me. I'll trade my fantasy football for romantic ecstasy any day! *That is a winning season.*

For Mars Man: Enjoy sex. Between you as married people it is as honest and pure as the freshly fallen snow. So you don't have to think of it as being nasty and treat it as a $25 fling with a $50 hooker. What goes on in your marriage bed is holy and good. It is only when we pervert it that it becomes perverted. Remember, just as we are "get to the point" people, our spouses are not. Remember they work in 4-D and not 2-D as we. They are interested in the way we are feeling and they want to know that we are interested in how they feel. Take your time. We are not running with the bulls at Pamplona! *Sex is not just the orgasmic feeling we get, it is the intimacy of speech, the closeness of body, and the eye to eye honesty that this act alone can bring. Take your time. Wallow in it. Bask. Open your eyes - it aint just about Mr. Happy!*

For Venus Woman: Do not think that what you are participating in is somehow something to be ashamed of. This is a *God creative* act. This act, from the beginning was the design of the greatest Creator of all. Enjoy. Rejoice. Cry. Scream for joy. It is good! Look deeply into your spouses eyes and see his soul. Co-share the amazing bond that you have and realize that this is making your marriage stronger and your relationship more complete.

For Both Planets: I wish to again overtly dispel the perception that sex is dirty. I have to reiterate this because the media constantly reiterates a skewed view. I don't think I could stress this enough! Within the marriage bond sex is totally AWESOME. Let's look at a few choice responses to different scenarios. A few guys (and often girls) see a pregnant girl across the street. They know her to be single. They say, "She got Knocked up." I know it is a guttural slang, but allow me to make a point. There was a movie with that title, although I have not seen it. On the other hand, when you see an obviously married person sporting a lower tummy you say, "Awe... your going to have a baby! Congratulations! I'm so excited for you." If you are one who is somehow mentally brow beat by the fact that you are enjoying sex... quit. It is a God designed act within marriage. I believe He would be disappointed if you didn't. I believe He wants us to take full advantage of everything He has for us. This includes great sex.

My Advice

Come to understand that a key to great sex is time. The Biblical lover took time to set up his lover with words of enchantment and endearment. He walks with her in the morning, and strolls with her in the afternoon, sits beside her to watch a sunset, and goes leisurely to climbing trees and squeezing pomegranates and enjoying the splendor of the Mountain of Myrrh. He does this act of love until the dawn breaks! The morning! *They must have had some pre-Viagra herbal extract back then... wow. I've got to read through Song of Solomon more often!* Men... do you want great sex? Slow down! Sex is not supposed to be the racetrack where we see how fast we can get through the quarter mile. Treat this act like the Indy 500. Pace yourself for a long race, it takes stamina, it takes endurance, but victory lap is worth it. I'm not saying that every time has to be a marathon, we all like to drive the sprint cars, ladies too from time to time, but it should not be standard.

One More For Mars Man: Slow down there speed racer. Enjoy the garden stroll. Smell the roses. take your time to let nature build to it's fullest expectation. Look openly into the eyes of your beloved and seek to please her with the same vigor that you want to be pleased. Never pervert the occasion by bringing foreign material into this marriage bed. Do not come to this bed with a filthy video on your mind. Come to this bed with nothing but her on your mind. Make this a holy moment.

One More For Venus Woman: Help your spouse know what you enjoy. Speak to him softly and do not bring to this bed expectations from pornographic stimuli that you have seen throughout the day on television shows or soaps either.

2.10

FRIENDLY PLANETS

How do you stop a Man from choking? Take your foot off of his neck.

This is so much a part of the last chapter, but I felt that the last chapter was getting a little to long, so if you haven't thrown this book away as heresy, let me go another step with you. Another key to exquisite sex is safety. The rush of a dangerous situation may be exciting to you, but not to your spouse! I speak to both of you here. If somehow sex has to be outside of the boundaries of privacy and security, than there are most likely other issues that need to be addressed in your life and psyche. Have you ever seen a couple having sex in public? I have. Somehow the openness of watching a couple "do it" in the seat next to me in the *Amtrack* coach car gave sex a nasty perception. *Not that I was watching… it was tough not to notice… and hear.* It looked more like two animals in heat rather than two lovers consummating their passion. Seeing two individuals so open and so given toward exhibitionism made me feel as if the sex was not actually between them, but maybe it was also somehow between me too. Great sex is discreet. Great sex is this holy act between three; you, your spouse, and God. Yes God. Give your partner the security to know that this act of love is so reserved and so protected and so special, that you would not risk anyone else being given the opportunity to see it. Anything shy of this is pornography. It is perversion. Adultery.

Knowing that our intimacy is reserved for me alone is of great treasure to my heart. Knowing that it is not a reenactment of some pornography gives me the ability to be feel safe and secure in Mike's arms. –Terica Williams

I know that some of you Men and maybe a few Women enjoy the rush of danger. We all do at times! The movies have portrayed to us that the more obscure or risky the place of intercourse the better it is. There is not a person in the United States who by the age of eighteen hasn't heard the term *The Mile High Club*. To be honest, it does sound rather intriguing. On the other hand, I have not found the airline restrooms to be all that clean nor roomy enough to really enjoy a bathroom *potty* experience much less a frolic of sexual exploration. Some have said the rush from this particular act is from the lack of oxygen at the higher altitude. Well maybe one might prefer to just enjoy each other in a similar situation like the trunk of a car with duct tape over their face, not to mention that I believe you can be arrested for either. If you have perverted your mind so badly that the only way you can "get your groove on" is to find voyeuristic exhilaration, I would really suggest that you work through the bonding issues discussed in part one of this book, repent, and go to *real* good counselor.

Why can't we be friends?

I love to listen to comedy. It is my weakness. maybe it is because of my career path, maybe it is because I just really love to laugh. To illustrate a point I go to my mental archive of comedians. It was on XM radio, which by the way I am featured on daily myself (shameless plug), that I heard a young comedian by the name of Mike Birbiglia. He described a scene in which he was watching some HBO, Cinemax, or Showtime documentary about sex. He described in detail the very pornographic act that this group of couples was participating in. He then began to banter about what is going to happen when these perverts come to there senses in a few years and wonder what in the world they were doing on national television before millions of people. He laughingly chided about their embarrassment that would surely follow when they come to their senses. Here's the deal… What this Sodom and Gomorra world promotes only brings shame in the long run. What you have been programmed to believe is acceptable will one day be a tape you wish never existed. I wonder how many girls who have "Gone Wild" for the camera will one day carry the guilt and shame as their children see what Mom or Dad was really all about. Your sexual escapades are designed to be so special that it would be reserved for none other than your spouse. One of the "Big Ten" as we call it at home is to Remember the Sabbath and keep it holy. I wish that you would add an eleventh; Remember the marriage bed and keep it holy. Holy is so good that once experienced would never be replaced by unholy.

I want my children to know that their parents enjoy a healthy sexual experience that has been reserved totally and exclusively for each other. I want them to see sex as a great and awesome act carried out between two people who love each other deeply and our fully committed to each other alone. It is an act of unity. It is an act of bonding between souls. Sex is clean and wholesome when it happens between husband and wife.
–Terica Williams

For Mars Man: Don't buy into the worlds view of sex as a pornographic act of voyeurism or eroticism. That kind of sex is nothing more than perversion. Retrain yourself to see sex as holy and keep it as one would treasure a fine jewel. If you love your spouse you will want to protect her from exposure to the elements. Love your spouse.

For Venus Woman: Stand your ground on this! Don't become jaded by the medias portrayal of *Sex in the City* or the *Desperate Housewives* it creates. Who really wants desperation when you can have spiritual, emotional, and physical ecstasy?

For Both Planets: Remember the marriage bed and keep it holy. Anything less is wantonly bringing adultery into your marriage. Now depending upon how you interpret the word *adultery* that could be grounds Biblical grounds for divorce. I know that is tough talk… and that is why I left it to your interpretation. In High School when we saw our fellow students hot and heavy in the school yard somebody would always shout, "GET A ROOM!"

2.11

PUT YOUR HUBBLE TELESCOPE AWAY

Men get jealous more often, but Women can when get demented sometimes, and for weird reasons. I never thought about that until I got married, and one day my wife came home from work and was mad at me because there was a pretty Woman on the bus she thought I would have liked. –Ray Romano

Another key to excellent sex is to avoid *all* pornography. Some of you will call me a prude here. Okay. Go ahead. Now let's look at the pro's and con's of this statement. Some might argue that "the Bible says the marriage bed is undefiled," and try to turn that verse into something it is not. The bed is undefiled, but our minds unfortunately are not. Early in our marriage I made a decision that said this: On nights that I see some television movie where I find myself in some strange way physically attracted to the leading lady, I will not have sex. It has stemmed from this idea. I did not want to go to bed with my wife while my mind somehow secretly made love to Julia Roberts! Every Man reading this understands my statement and I'll bet every Woman does too. Is my desire to be wholly devoted unto my wife a silly notion? Ask her if she thinks so. Ask any Woman if they would be pleased or disappointed with that kind of devotion. *I could be wrong.* Maybe we all prefer to be used as a blow up doll for an imaginary hollywood hunk?

> *Staying faithful doesn't just involve not sleeping with someone other than your spouse. It means putting your best effort and energy into enhancing the romance you have with your mate. Faithfulness is more than just saying "no" to others; it's also saying "yes" to your spouse.*
> *–Steve & Annie Chapman*

I believe many of our problems within sexual fulfillment and our own inhibitions in sex can be traced back to our own minds and our predisposition about what sex looks like, and who it looks like with. Pornography has been designed by its producers to demonstrate to you things that could never be done in real life, at least not without the help of extra people in the room with lighting, music, air brushes, and *fanny* photo doubles. Flying back and forth from *Los Angeles* every other week or so I have had the opportunity to sit next to a few of these "so-called" sex symbols. *Let me tell you that make-up and hair stylists have been very good to them.* Let me illustrate it another way. If I go to Disney's MGM studios I can watch them film on a soundstage something that looks completely different on the film. The action, the camera angles, the music by John Williams (no relation to me), and the incredibly good looking actors, are all designed to give me the perception that what I am seeing is really happening. It is a set up. Pornography ruins the humor and spontaneity of wholesome sex. It does this by creating false scenarios that our minds die trying to recreate! Men leave their wives because they cannot experience what they think they would experience if they only did it "this way" or another.

> *I'm very loyal in a relationship, all relationships. When I'm with my mother, I don't look at other moms, "Wow... I wonder what her macaroni and cheese taste like." –Gary Shandling*

I am fortunate to be able to say that I never got involved with the whole internet porn scene. I was spared from that and I pray that I will always be able to say that. To say that it has not caused me to wonder would be a falsehood. In my counseling with its victims, I have found the strength to refuse to click on. I have friends who are recovering from it and friends who have not yet recovered. However, I can take you back to a page from a porno magazine when I was in high school that I found on a fishing trip. I can still see the picture and hear the voice (though just in print) of this very-very voluptuous totally nude Woman describing what she wanted to do to me. *Maybe I should actually say "What the writers said she wanted to do to me." Looking back I doubt that this poor misled bimbo could even articulate the concept of gravity.* It has been twenty-five years and I can still see it like it was yesterday. How can anybody live up to what airbrush technology can do with a body? How can Solomon in all of his verbiage live up to Photoshop and a staff of writers bent on making me squirm in my fifteen year old seat? Men listen, you cannot expect to get a good meal at home if you are going to spend the day at the snack machine! As a relatively fat Man I understand this analogy and I'll bet you do too.

> *Quit window shopping. It only leads to disappointment and adultery. Learn to love the one your with.*

Now let me speak to the Women about this for a minute. You must quit the pornography too! Let me expound on the definition of pornography for a moment. Whereas Men are stimulated by the undressed body, and many Women are too, Women are more often stimulated by the undressed emotion. So the difference in Men and Women's pornography could be described with the definition: *Emotion driven fantasy vs. visual driven fantasy.* Women's pornography can often enough be the paperback romance novels, the Soaps, the sexually perverted television shows, and even the movies that some people want to refer to as "chick flicks." Pornography does not have to have visual nudity in it to do damage. A husband may be stimulated by a poster of the Hooters Girls, while his wife is being manipulated by the words on a page of a *Harlequin Romance* or a *Gossip Girl* novel. From the time our Venus Women were little girls they have been moved by the story (words) delivered in gloriously intimate innuendo. Words have been their friend. Their verbal pornography rips at the foundation of their marriage in the same way the Man's visual pornography does.

I had a Man in my office the other day and he said, "My wife made a millionaire out of me." I asked him, "What were you before?" He said, "A multi-millionaire." –Dr. Phil

When I articulated the pressure for a Woman to live up to what the porn industry has placed as a sexual gold standard the Ladies reading this book more than likely nodded an approval, or maybe even voiced a hearty "Amen!" Well… treat the Men with the same respect. You do not want to live up sexually to *Debbie Does Dallas*, likewise Men do not want to try and live up to the writing staff of *Desperate Ho-wives*. Yes I spelled it *Ho-wives* on purpose. It was not a typo. Nobody can live up to a *Ho-llywood* stunt show. We would run out of words. Remember? We have a job and responsibilities. We cannot sit in the garden and have tea all day and hold you, and caress you the way you deserve to be held and caressed. The lawn needs to be mowed, and you want us to paint the living room again. Come to think of it, you don't have the time either. The baby is crying in the other room, dinner is on the stove, and you have got to get the older kids to little league! I am not trying to break anyones mental bubble, only to remind you that pornography, which is for both parties is mutually destructive. Likewise, you ladies cannot hold your husband up to this standard and not have to live up to the standards that his version of pornography has created.

The happiness of your life depends on the quality of your thoughts: therefore, guard accordingly, and take care that you entertain no notions unsuitable to virtue and reasonable nature. –Marcus Aurelius

Did you notice that I argued this point on purely emotional grounds? I could have argued it from a Biblical basis, but I know Biblical congruity is not always the basis of every persons world. I could argue until the cows come home from a biblical perspective (check out *all* the verses listed at the back of this book). Adultery is not always an affair carried out… most often adultery sneaks into a marriage as an affair of the mind. Nevertheless it is still adultery. It is still a poison to the bond. It is still just as detrimental to a great relationship and great sex as a weekend fling with your boss or secretary. I want to suggest a book entitled *Every Man's Battle* for every Man who has any struggle in this area.

Here's A Stick In your eye

I live in airports. There are few places I know (other than the internet) that you can watch up close and personal voluptuous Women and dark sexy Men in their native suggestive habitat. I have walked past shoe shine shops with Women lifted high in the air with their legs spread to get shoe shine. The truth is they were nothing more than hurting females trying to fulfill their needs through their own exhibitionism. Voyeurism! If I had a dollar for every time some bra-less female bent over the seat in front of me with her blouse open to her navel, I would not have to try and make money hocking books about the subject! I wish I could say that as a Christian Man that I find that unattractive or at least not interesting at all to me. I do not understand Mans seemingly helpless attraction to the *two twins!* I recognize it is there. So does every advertising agency in the country. Right or wrong - it is there. So what is a Man to do.

In my effort to keep my mind completely true to my wife, I bought a pair of reading glasses. They are not specifically for reading. They are for blurring. Quit laughing and follow along with me. When I feel that there are days when I might be tempted to risk bringing adulterous thoughts into my worlds I put on the reading glasses. Now everything in front of me is a blur! I can still maneuver through the airport, but I cannot see the details around me. This is not a new idea. The devout Jew often walked with his head down so as not to be attracted by the opposite sex. Is that prudish? Whatever! I call it protection.

Yes… It may be prudish…but I'm in good company… Jesus certainly was. I believe that he said if your eye causes you to sin, that you should poke it out. He declared that it was better for you to go to heaven blind than go to hell with your sight. *I guess He didn't fully understand grace?* Yes that was sarcasm mixed with truth none the less. I might be a prude, but my family is too important to me to risk them to an affair of the heart, the mind, or the penis.

Remember that it is not just the peak of the mountains that is alluring to the climber. A climber loves the foothills too. Dress in a way that says you are not even looking for new climbers. I know that our bodies are Gods creation, but the Christ follower has a goal to help keep everyone looking forward to seeing Jesus more than seeing a glimpse of your cleavage. –Terica Williams

---

For Mars Man: Learn to turn your head. You can do it. Make it a challenge to yourself to see how many times this week you can turn your head instead of trying to see how much more you can see. Try it for thirty days. Go on a breast fast! Pass the T-back test. Call a moratorium on window shopping. Conversely you will also find your wife's body that much more intriguing.

For Venus Woman: It is not that much different for you. I don't know what really turns you on. I'm pretty sure it is not the rolls around my belly. Will you call yourself to the same standard that you would love to have from the Man you love? How would that make you feel to know that your husband so loved you and valued his relationship to you that he lived in strict focus on you? Treat him the same way. Be the example. teach your children well.

Do not cause another to stumble. It would be better for an anchor to be hung around your neck and you be tossed into the sea. –Matthew 18:6

For Both Planets: The way you dress is often a tell tale sign as to how you value mental fidelity in a marriage. If your desire as a Woman is to show your well pleasing stuff to other Men, I'm telling you right now you are helping other Men commit adultery in their mind. Set the example of prudent Women. You can ride on the "Well if Men weren't so horny that they couldn't look at half my cleavage without lusting…" excuse if you want to. It won't hold up in Heaven's court. Can I remind you what Jesus said as to those who would cause another to stumble? I'm sure your familiar with the concept, and I will let it go at that. If advertising your wears didn't effect Men, the television ads wouldn't use them. It is an axiom. I'm sorry. I believe you should have the right to go topless without being lusted after… and If you move to Africa you can have that freedom. Move to Africa and you can burn your shirt, your bra, and run sticks through your nipples. *But you aren't in Africa!* Even if you were there we would find little boys in our country looking at you in *National Geographic* and lusting.

Now we don't want to hear from *Him* on this one! High fashion is not what you will stand before God for. His standard for all of our dress would be considerate of others… and not ourselves. Please give us sexually supercharged Men a hand and just button up on extra button. If one extra button is detracting from your beauty, then you really need a complete makeover. Who wants to be only attractive for something that is going to be gone in a few years. I've never met a lady at a nursing home and said, "She may be wearing a diaper now… but you should have seen her when she was young." We all love the godly Woman and Godly Gentleman who sits there waiting for the old gospel ship to pick them up and take them home.

> ### *Modesty is very alluring. When will the contemporary female catch on to this? –Gordon Douglas*

Did I let Men off the hook here? No. I certainly think Men need to dress modestly too. We all know you have a [package] to display, so you don't have to sling it from your speedo at the pool. You are a Man. We know! Contemporary media has turned many a Venus Woman into a butt watcher. It was only natural that as the world itself became more overtly and indiscriminately sexual that this would come. Welcome to the new age. Upon understanding what also stimulates a female, I think it would behoove Men to mind their flirtatious words and keep their flowery compliments for their Wives. That is just my opinion… I could be wrong. What do I know? I'm just a Man. I will dig into this in a few more paragraphs for the Men… their time is coming. Remember that modesty is very appealing and your goal as a married person is to limit your sex appeal to that of your husband.

2.12

OWN A TWO SEATER ROCKET

The billionaire who married a young blonde model died. After his death she had three days of mourning followed by several months of shopping.
–Ken Davis

The number one key to fantastic sex is to make it totally exclusive! Sex should be, undoubtedly understood, that it is a privilege given to one person and one person only... the spouse. Now you might think that this is just another way to say what I just said. Whatever! I want to offer a preemptive strike on whatever could possibly be thrown at you. Skip this chapter if you must.

My wife once asked me If I knew how to dance. This hurt my feelings because we were dancing when she asked me. –Emo Philips

Knowing that this holy action (sex) is not available to the highest bidder, even if that bidder is Richard Geer or Leonardo DeCaprio, or Brittany Spears, or Amy Grant, *or even Boy George* brings sacredness to this amazing gift called sex. Exclusivity is also very appealing. Exclusivity is very intriguing. The understanding of exclusivity comes on the tales of our last point in that the exclusivity is also honored in the mind. Sex was designed to be a personal and private act and not open to others Take a minute a read Hebrews 13:4. Go ahead... look it up... this chapter can wait.

When a woman steals your husband, there is no better revenge than to let her keep him. –Cecile Kaiser

How does one such as yourself advertise at work and in the marketplace? Do you present yourself as exclusive? Men, does the way you talk and what you talk about lead other Women to *even guess* you could be snagged? Ladies, does the clothing you wear show just enough of your goodies to make other Men think they might be available for shared usage? *Are you a single family dwelling or a time share?* Advertisements are a good way to tell what is in the store! If you need to strut your stuff before others, I've got a good idea that you have got some problems in your own heart, and that problem is not your spouse... it is you.

In some parts of the world a man doesn't know his wife until he marries her. Our own country is definitely in that category! –Bradley Bean

Flirting is dangerous at worst, and lying at best. If it is lived out it becomes the poison of your relationship or the relationship of another human being who deserves to be treated as respectfully as you. If it is just *teasing*, than it is really a *lie* cloaked in fantasy and has no business in a believers vocabulary or really any other ethical persons life. I have a feeling that those who are flirtatious in their sexual escapades, suggestive words, or dress are actually dealing with other emotional issues of acceptance and need to spend some time with a professional on this matter. *Call a good counselor today.*

The world is flat, right?

Let me be honest with you. I don't consider myself a real catch. There was a time in my youth when Women might have looked at me as being pretty hot, but I'm sure that even that is just a figment of my imagination. Nevertheless, I often find myself in positions at my own shows where there are females who seem rather flirtatious. Yes, I may be the typical Man who is trying to feel good about himself. I don't think so. The truth is that [authority and personality] brings out the stalkers, the freaks, and the needy. *Not to mention that my amazing sense of humor is listed as a desire on every singles add in the country! Yes, again that was a joke.* I too have to deal with those who are *so emotionally needy* that they would throw themselves even at the guy who is teaching on this subject. *There are a lot of needy people out there. I hope you are not one of them. If you are, let me remind you that I live in a gated and guarded community and my wife knows how to use a gun.* We are in an age where almost every Pastor I know has to deal with this too. Some have had to hire body guards just to protect this area alone in their ministry. Guard your heart, mind, emotion, words, and desires.

> *Curiosity has killed more marriages than cats.* –Dave Davidson

---

For Mars Man: Having a picture of your Wife and kids on your desk is not enough. Some predator type Women are actually allured by your marital fidelity and excited by the desire to have it in their own life. I want to suggest to you that you learn to keep a healthy distance. Do not let the females (and lately also males for that matter) get close enough to be dangerous. This may seem standoffish. Whatever. I would rather seem standoffish then have to explain to my children why Daddy won't be living at home anymore. I would rather seem standoffish than have to tell my Wife that I had an affair and that now she has inadvertently been exposed to an STD. *It sounds rather obvious when you look at the "Murphy's Law" implications doesn't it?*

For Venus Woman: Having a picture of your Husband and kids on your desk is not enough either. Do your co-workers (male and female) know of your undying devotion to your spouse. I hope that you have put in place firm boundaries that do not allow you to be sucked into the trap of the enemy of your marriage. If you ever have to sit and counsel a Mother who has to tell her Husband and two Children that she had a *quickie affair*... and now has AIDS... you will understand and support every word I said. You'd probably put a bumper sticker about it on your car too.

For Both Planets: There is no room for error here! Make a vow to yourself and to your spouse that you have reserved yourself (eyes, hands, heart, mind, emotion, body) purely for them. Hold this to be the "Great Unshakeable-Unbreakable" in your life. Live in a way that clearly creates a florescent line in the sand that is clearly seen by all who pass your way.

2.13

TO THE MOON ALICE

The quarrels of lovers are like summer storms. Everything is more beautiful when they have passed. –Suzanne Necker

It was only in this past decade that I began to hear or at least remember to have heard the term *passive-aggressive*. *Passive-aggressive* sounded a lot like an oxymoron. You know - two incongruent terms. Like jumbo-shrimp, military-intelligence, rap-music, or United-Methodist. *All my Methodist friends understand what I mean there, for the rest of you just use the first three illustrative examples.* I have come to realize that I am often stricken with this condition! In fact you might say it runs in my family. I don't know precisely where I picked it up. I have not been sharing needles, and I certainly always use the protective paper toilet seat covers at the airport restrooms. I will admit to an occasional battle with Athlete's foot... but this? How did I get this... this... personality disorder? Can I even call it a personality disorder? I'm sure I will get clarification letters from you counselor types. *Let it go. Walk away.* Let me define it as I have come to know it. Understand this is my street level definition taken not from a medical journal but rather from experience in dealing with it. *Passive aggressive syndrome is the act of treating a person poorly without dealing with what is really bothering you about that person.* It is often voiced as laziness being used in an aggressive manner! It is LOUD DEMONSTRATIVE APATHY! Now I am going to look it up in the dictionary and see how close I came at my attempt to define the word. While I search the net, which we all know is the most reliable place to find information, take this time to stop and get a refreshing drink of Coffee, Tea, or your favorite bottled water. *I like Aquafina the best.*

There is no way under the sun of making a Man worthy of love, except by loving him. –Thomas Merton

Okay I'm back. Did you enjoy your drink? According to the web (thestraightdope.com), PAPD as it is often abbreviated was first introduced in a 1945 U.S. War Department technical bulletin, describing soldiers who weren't openly insubordinate but shirked duty through procrastination, willful incompetence, and so on. After the war the term found its way into civilian psychiatric practice and for many years was listed in the Diagnostic and Statistical Manual, the bible of the mental health trade. According to the revised third edition (DSM-III-R, 1987), someone had PAPD if he displayed five or more of the following behaviors: (1) procrastinates, (2) sulks or argues when asked to do something he doesn't want to do, (3) works inefficiently on unwanted tasks, (4) complains without justification of unreasonable demands, (5) "forgets" obligations... The list goes on and on.

Wow, you have just described every teenager in America! The problem is that many of us have come to live our married lives in passive aggressiveness toward each other We may not be as blatant as the military description, but our actions and reactions expressed to our spouse seems to say that we could not care any less about them than we do right now including our relationship to them. What a tragedy? The more clinical definition suggests this type of behavior manifests itself to become among worst of all spousal aggression. It is an aggression tantamount to saying that "You don't really even exist enough to care." I have heard it voiced that the greatest degree of hatred is the point at which the other party is ignored and treated as if they did not even exist. Curse me, slap me, call me stupid, but at least acknowledge my existence! It breaks my heart, but I have to confess that I have demonstrated this PAPD at times in my own marriage.

> *Man is a clever animal who often behaves like an imbecile.*
> *–Albert Schweitzer*

Mars Men are well adept at PAPD! We demonstrate it in our daily life and even more noticeably in our lack of actions. Could we describe it as *angry-apathy?* Many have reached a point where we have chosen to simply non-peacefully coexist with a spouse rather than fight to make what could be great... great! Mere coexistence is the pinnacle of PAPD as you see that there is a problem, but not mustering the effort needed to climb the hill and win the battle. So the battles of our married life become daily skirmishes fought over insignificant issues rather than the real issues. Our responses to each other become short words of bitterness wrapped up in answers to questions that aren't even being asked.

> *Webster wrote the dictionary because of his wife. Everything he would say, she would say, "What's that supposed to mean?" –Jeff Allen*

There are many ways a Mars Man uses this passive aggression on Venus Women, but none more effectively than in the areas of overlooking her emotional makeup. The unwillingness to actively participate in meeting your spouse's emotional needs among the highest examples of PAPD that a Man can express to a Woman. This can ruin any relationship... and do it quickly. Keep pushing this envelope and you will find yourself communicating by envelope through a lawyer and a check.

Venus Women also have an excellent (if I may use that adjective so positively) mode of operation in their use of PAPD, not the least of which is displayed in the bedroom. Not that there are not other ways in which Women can display it, but that is definitely hitting a Man where it hurts. A sexually frustrated Man will find it hard to be all that he can be in a marriage. Keep turning the thumb screws on this one and you will get more than you bargained for from the lion! Backhanded comments that claw at a male ego (especially in front of others), has been the cause of many a marriage ruination.

The husband should fulfill his marital duty to his wife, and likewise the wife to her husband. The wife's body does not belong to her alone but also to her husband. In the same way, the husband's body does not belong to him alone but also to his wife. Do not deprive each other except by mutual consent and for a time, so that you may devote yourselves to prayer. Then come together again so that Satan will not tempt you because of your lack of self-control.
–1 Corinthians 7:3-5

I would rather see a couple get verbally loud and direct, using boisterous words, than try to get a point across to one another of their disappointment using a weapon of passivity. Let me say to the 50% of those who read this book and claim to be Christ followers, that you cannot justifiably use passive aggression. Your own Lord does not allow it. You must reach terms of agreement and disagreement on honest and open terms. You are not allowed to fight your battles in a backhanded way. Vengeance is not yours to give. Be Man enough and Woman enough to talk to your spouse without dealing back-handed blows. Consider how you can stir each other up to love. *Hey I think that is a verse somewhere! I wonder where? Could it be the Bible?* Let our godliness begin at home. Damnation upon the years I personally wasted giving perfect strangers the best that Mike Williams had to offer.. only to come home to give my wife the moldy leftovers. *Shame on me. Shame on me.*

We learn from our mistakes... well... hopefully we do. Especially if we are smart enough not to repeat them. That is just the way it is. Each time we repeat a mistake we dig a deeper rut in which to rise from. I'm no farmer... but thats a tough row to hoe.

Much of the passive aggressiveness we see demonstrated is just a response to a past passive aggressive statement, which was a response to another past passive aggressive action, which was definitely a knee-jerk response to another passive aggressive action. Do you see how it goes on and on like Domino's? *Ray Charles can see that my friends.* What we are going to do about it?

Shut up and listen

I wish to take a phrase from one of my favorite musical composers, Michael W. Smith (no relation to me... especially seeing that we have different last names). Michael wrote, "How long will we drink from the chalice of indifference... and neither be hot or be cold?" *He mumbled the next lines so I do not know what he said exactly, but it sounded like he said, "sober-sno-benose." I really doubt that was what he meant to say.* I believe that many a Mars Man and Venus Woman resorts to drinking from the chalice of indifference in their marriage relationship. This is a result of having given up. They lack the ability (at least in their own mind) to communicate (remember that communication by definition goes two ways) to this *other world* being, or after long trial have come to believe it is impossible, and thus shrivel into passive aggression.

For Mars Man: Women see passive aggressiveness in simple things. Your lack of fulfilling everyday culturally male jobs is considered by your spouse as a backhanded slap to her face. Is that what you were going for? Yes? Then you are a cowardly Man to say the least. I had a much better adjective to use their but the publisher made me take it out! Let's level the playing field. In fact let's quit treating our fights as if there is a winner or loser. Let's see the enemy as *anything that does not strengthen the bond between you*. You may win the argument and get your way, and get to do your thing, but did your marriage win? If your marriage didn't win - you lost also my testosterone toting friend. You may have all the testosterone in the world, enough to bottle and sell it. Impressive. You may beat your chest and roar. *Scary! Scary!* BUT YOU STILL LOST! It doesn't matter how many shots Michael Jordan gets through the hoop... if he doesn't get enough to win... he has lost. There are so many good illustrations from the Bible as to how to treat your wife. I simply ask you to read them. If you are among those who call yourself a follower of Christ, you might want to take a few of them to heart. *Now that was beyond sarcasm... it was just plain true.*

For Venus Woman: I want to drop a new word on you. I made it up myself. Are you ready? *Nag-attude!* There it is. Men hate what they perceive as nag-attude. Properly explained it could best be defined as *arguing or complaining with a condescending attitude*. I'm sure that nobody reading this book has ever done that, so just read this so you might help others. When you need to approach a Man with an issue, do it without sarcasm, shame, or ridicule. Ask him how you should feel about the issue or situation. Put the question in his court. Do this without yelling. Do this without bringing past mistakes he has made into the discussion. Last weeks events are gone. You have not seen a referee throw a flag on a ball player, and then site him for a foul in an earlier game, or even an earlier quarter. Don't you do it. Men [though vaguely] can remember their past mistakes, and most likely you will get more points across by them knowing that you remember, but honoring them in not bringing it up. Share without attitude. Honor a Man as the head of the home whether or not he is acting like it. If we impeached the President out every time he messed up, we would be getting a new President every week. Maybe every day. Hourly? *You interpret that any way you want.* Please share honestly and openly with your husband in a time when you can have his full attention. Make an appointment if you have to. Do you have a calendar? *Google will provide you one free online.*

For Both Planets: People fight in improper manners when they quit fighting *for the marriage* and start *fighting their partner*. Did you hear that? I will repeat it! People fight in improper manners when they quit fighting *for the marriage* and start *fighting their partner*. When will you quit fighting for yourself, your rights, your freedom, and start fighting for the common good? You can passive aggressively try to change your partner for the rest of your marriage. *Good luck!* Waste your time if you want. No genuinely wise individual would do that. It's time you, like the prodigal son, "GOT SANE" again in this area!

2.14

AMATEUR INTERPLANETARY PROBLEM SOLVERS

Opinions are like hind quarters, everybody has them, and many of them stink.

This is going to be short so listen up. The girls at the office and the guys at the job site more than likely know less about marriage than you, although they are more than willing to offer the depth of their wisdom-less knowledge with you. People love to give their opinion. Most of the advice you will get from your work buddies and often your church buddies stinks! It ruins marriages! It wrecks families. The last thing you need to do is fill your mind with bad spices and cheap condiments. No matter how few hot peppers you put in the stew, it still makes it *too spicy* for most. *All the A-1 steak sauce in the world will not fix it.* A little bit of arsenic can ruin an entire flask of sweet tea. *It can also kill your spouse… so don't get any ideas… at least until the insurance is paid up.* Jesus said it eloquently when he said, "A little mold ruins the whole loaf". In other words, a little bad advice can ruin good intentions.

> *Don't push your husband toward an affair at the office. You be the one he finds under his desk! You be the one who pursues him and tells him that he is desired. Within the bounds of privacy, chase him where you can. This is a guy who grew up with fantasy. He has had dreams about this kind of tom-foolery… and at one time you were the star of those dreams. Keep the dream alive! –Terica Williams*

For Mars Man: Tom, Dick, and Harry are not marriage experts. Most of the *dung* they espouse is made up on the spot. *Do you not know that 86% of all statistics are created at the time of a conversation? That statistic certainly was.* Listen to those you know to have a great marriage. Look at the all-stars. That is those who have been married for fifty years or more… happily. Seek godly counsel from them.

For Venus Woman: Desperate Housewives begets *desperate* housewives. To think that you can get godly information from the average person on the street would be foolish beyond foolish. These are not stock tips we are talking about… this is your marriage. It's success or failure relies much upon you. Would you go to an Optometrist if you found a lump on your breast? Would you call a plumber if your tire was flat? If you said yes, close this book right now and call your lawyer… and by all means don't procreate… ever!

Okay, you have to talk to someone. You are a talker by nature. I understand. Find someone who has a track record of success in marriage…. fifty years in the making. Fifty godly years under their belt. Find people who believe that divorce is not a *great and quick* solution. Start your conversation with "What has God been teaching you this week?" You certainly want someone who is engaged in current relations with the Almighty. Ask them for a few Bible verses to back up anything they say. Then and only then, seek advice for being a better partner, and not only advice on how to make your partner better for you. Misery tends to love company. Much of what is given as counsel is simply bitterness being allowed to live to fight another day… through you. Did you get that? That was a little tougher than the first analogy.

For Both Planets: If you need help, go to the source. Do you and your spouse ever pray together? No? *"You sissy!"* Yes I have resorted to name calling. Back to the point. It is no shame to get some godly help. Start out by finding a good Christian counselor who believes that Biblical counseling might be at least a little better than contemporary *Freudian* bull droppings that blame everything on a perverted attraction to ones mother. Find a counselor who is experiencing a happy marriage. Find one who can say the tough stuff. Be Man and Woman enough to listen to them. Work first to become the best spouse you can be, then and only then can you righteously help your spouse become all that they can be. Until you are whole, your expectations for your spouse will always be rather skewed and your marriage will end up rather screwed. *That rhymed.*

2.15

BUT NOW YOU LIVE ON EARTH

To want what I have... to take what I'm given with grace... for this I pray... on my wedding day. –Don Henley

I don't know about you, but no matter how much I may think I have been wronged, or wrongly treated by my spouse, I can tell you I have treated my spouse wrongly. No matter how much our spouse deserved it, we have responded in ways that are inappropriate for a believer to act. In fact, I would say we have responded in ways that are inappropriate for anyone to act. *Men... this is where the rubber meets the road. Ladies... this is where the powder touches the nose.* I am going to make a statement that cannot be overlooked. I am going to make a statement that unless understood, grasped, and followed will inadvertently doom your marriage to failure. A statement that is so powerful I would say that if you cannot grasp it, you should just give up now and find something else to do with your life. Have I made myself clear yet? This is a biggie! It wouldn't be saved for the end unless it was the orgasmic climactic wisdom of the entire part 2. That biggie can best be summed up in one word: FORGIVENESS!

> *If I could not forgive Mike for the way he has hurt me over the years, and he could not forgive me for the way I have hurt him over the years, our marriage would be in sad shape. It might not be together at all. Anytime you have two people, even though those people are unified, there will be hurts. You must accelerate the forgiveness within a marriage. Make it a foundational cornerstone building block in your marriage. –Terica Williams*

As believers we have been called to be citizens of a different world. We have been called to walk in demonstration of a heavenly kingdom in this present world while we wait for His kingdom to wonderfully come. We have been asked to be peculiar people... not by a tattoo or uniform, and not by secret handshake or salute. The Bible says that they (this seems to be speaking of those real people around us) would know we are Christ-like by our love. The ultimate demonstration of this love was declared to us in a simple sentence.

> *While we were yet fighting Him, He gave Himself in death to extend to us forgiveness. –Romans 5:8*

A marriage will not work without *forgiveness!* It cannot. It will not! *It can barely work with it!* It is a mandate for every believer to be, by example living out the life of Christ and the gift of God in forgiveness. You might squaller, "You don't know what this spouse has done…" That is right, I don't know! I don't know the pain. I don't know the agony. I don't know the guilt. I don't know the shame. I don't know the humiliation. I don't know the mess they have made. I don't know the jobs they have lost. I don't know about the drinking? I don't know about the pornography. *Need I go on?* All I do know is that you need to give forgiveness because God demands it. What is forgiveness? It is my giving up of the right to hate you, treat you poorly, awkwardly, improperly, disrespectfully, or passive-aggressively because of the action (or many actions) you have done… no matter how undeniably awful it was. GO BACK AND READ THIS PARAGRAPH AGAIN! NOW!

Forgive, and you shall be forgiven. –Luke 6:37

God demands forgiveness! *Demands* is a strong word. No passivity there boys! No passivity girls. I could list scripture after scripture on this one friends. I would bet that you could too. There is no verse in scripture or ancient text that declares that we have been given the option to opt out of forgiving… for any reason. I am not implying that a person in an abusive situation needs to stay in that situation. I am saying that for the health of the abused person, once they get to safety, they must come to a place of forgiveness for the abuser. This is as much about their own inner health as it is anything else. Yes there are Biblical grounds for divorce… but there are no Biblical grounds for continued hatred. We must forgive.

There is no remedy for sin(s) but to forgive!

So which comes first; the chicken or the egg? Well in this case the giving of forgiveness comes before the forgiveness. It seems to hold true throughout the entire Bible. It must be some sort of axiom don't you think? I must say that if there is one person in this entire world that I want forgiveness from it is God Almighty! How about you? I would certainly hate to allow some mere mortal to ruin my life here and my eternal life also. There's the ultimate double whammy! If I may use that *trite* term. Do you understand? I sincerely hope so.

In prayer there is a connection between what God does and what you do. You can't get forgiveness from God, for instance, without also forgiving others. –Matthew 6:14

There is a compelling story in the Matthew that tells of a person who had been forgiven of much who takes issue with another for their small debt. Jesus speaks to the issue and reminds the first person that they need to forgive with the same veracious forgiveness that they have received from God themselves. He wraps up the Matthew 18 chapter with the following words, "So likewise shall my heavenly Father do also unto you, if you from your hearts forgive not every one his brother their trespasses." Strong words! *I wish my publisher would spring for the money to put those in red. As you can see they didn't.*

I don't want a marriage that is made up of tolerance for the sake of the children. To leave a marriage in that condition is absurd and lazy. Both Men and Women need to work as hard at making the marriage great as they did at making the children. That alone would change half of the marriages in this world. The other half might have to work a little harder.

I am a huge Don Henley fan. *Don is the famed voice and front Man for the musical supergroup the Eagles. His solo career after the Eagles legendary breakup is what has drawn me to his exemplary talent. Yes… I know they have reunited. I no longer live under a rock!* I see very few contemporary writers who have been able to speak to such heavy subject matter in pathos filled musical voice as he. If you have not had a chance to listen to his last two solo disc's then you have truly missed a great-great experience. One of these masterpieces is entitled *Heart of The Matter*. Let me repeat a few lines:

> **We've got to get down**
> **to the heart of the matter**
> **It's about forgiveness**
> **Forgiveness**
> **Even if**
> **Even if**
> **You don't love me anymore**

Lyrics like that and some others that he has penned should elevate a person to musical sainthood. I on the other hand write songs about Waffle House waitresses and body-piercing gone bad. *I am ashamed of myself.*

I've heard that the human body is made up of 97% water. This means that the maximum difference that we can actually be from each other is 3% different… 3% aint that much when you think about it!

We are no longer strangers in a strange place. It is time that we begin to rethink this multiple planet thinking and start seeing ourselves as one. As a married person I understand that God now thinks of me and my spouse as one. Remember the *MAGIC* of the early verses this book quoted (Matthew 19:4-6)? We are not really from different planets, we just have been acting as though we are. We are all selfish mortals who from the time we were born have been crying out to have our own way, in our own time, and in our own space. The whole *rib experience* should illuminate to us that from the beginning we are an intrinsic part of each other. We all bleed red blood - we all cry salty tears. This road trip called life is not meant to be all about us. It is meant to be a mutual experience that is brought about to teach us how to live and love one another. Are we doing that? Are we walking each day in that illumination? Are we adapting to our surroundings in respect for each other and respect for the Creator? We must. So get over it.

However mean your life is, meet it and live it; do not shun it and call it hard names. It is not so bad as you are. It looks poorest when you are richest. The fault-finder will find faults even in Paradise. Love your life.
–Henry David Thoreau

For Mars Man: Lighten up. Nobody actually *pee'd in your Cheerios!* So stop making that face. You may be the Governor of your castle, but remember that your Governor's castle sits on property borrowed from the King. You are a master under the Master. You will give an account to Him! You are not your own, you have been bought with a price. Therefore live AND LOVE differently than the secular world does. You have been hurt? I am sorry. I really am. Welcome to planet Earth! It sucks down here at times. People (including spouses) will not always give you the respect you deserve, or want, or need. Get over it. Don't let the harboring of ill will cost you your marriage or the kingdom. Your spouse will not always treat you the way you feel you ought to be treated. Forgive! Forgive first. Let's be real honest, you do not always treat them with the utmost of care yourself. Right? Be honest.

You say to your children, "If Billy jumps off a bridge will you do it too?" Well teach by example. Do not return insult for insult. Return humility and love. Learn to take critique without having your dander up, or a chip on your shoulder. Demonstrate to your spouse the way that you should be treated by the way you treat them… and wait… yes wait… for the reciprocation. It may be a long time coming. Who cares? We are eternal beings. What is earthly time to *eternal lifers*?

Let me make a few more salient comments about this *Training - Taming* thing. Desire to be a little tamer and a little more trained. It is no shame to be domesticated. It means you get to eat food that is cooked, drive a car, and use the bathroom indoors. I have become quite partial to toilet paper over leaves. Call me *tame* or *trained*… I don't care… I *aint* going back to pooping in the woods. *I am addicted to Scott Tissue and Charmin on those rough days!*

For Venus Woman: Get your panties unwadded! *It is really uncomfortable to walk around that way.* I know you didn't wad them on purpose. It just happened. Walk in love and forgiveness… even when it hasn't been asked for… or deserved. There is little in this world that is actually deserved. If you and I rely on getting what we deserve in life it is going to be some pretty slim pickings in eternity. I am relying on grace. Not that I am not trying to be good, but that along with my effort out of love, I ask for mercy for that which I have missed. Forgive your spouse. Demonstrate how to be whole in yourself and He might just come along. Make his life so sweet that his every thought of you is that of honor and respect. That will pay off in the long haul. It did for my marriage.

For Both Planets: It will not work without forgiveness. We have all come too far and said too much. There has been so much water under the bridge that the well has run dry long ago. If there is going to be hope there has got to be forgiveness. We find ourselves at the same impasse some of us found ourselves at the closing of the bonding issues. What shall we do? It seems impossible. With Mars Man and Venus Woman it is… but with the new creation… it is possible to forgive! With God the impossible is possible. Marriages need miracles. I know that God is still performing miracles in the life of those who live according to His Holy Word.

My Prayer

May the God of Peace reign in our marriages.
May we be whole people that we may be honestly
bonded to each other.
May we allow Jesus to be the example by which
we learn to respond to one another.
May we give our lives in love and service for each other
as unto God himself.
May we continue in this process until He comes
to receive us unto Himself.
Amen and Amen.

2.16

A SPACE ODYSSEY OR LEGACY

Blessed is the person who walks through the desert and turns it into a well.
–Psalms 84:6

Well two days ago I finished what I believe may be my final edit of this book, sitting on a most uncomfortable wicker chair, during the wee hours of the morning, in my little room overlooking the ocean in the Dominican Republic. It has taken five years if you count the early drafts I threw away to get this far. I have come home from the D.R. to participate in the funeral of a dear friend and then leave with my family on vacation. It is here I sit at the kitchen table, computer powered up, with one more thing to say. It came to me while watching a movie last night and from some thoughts I had while giving the eulogy at the funeral. *So it's a double header.* Let's start with the movie. I'll bet you have already seen it.

Have you ever seen Apollo 13? You know the one with Tom Hanks. I think he is a great actor and desire him to play me if they ever make a movie about my life. *Some people say we look alike.* Now I have seen the movie before. We rented it years ago! *It is a good one!* It is a story of great failure that ends in great triumph. Like all really great movies it starts out with a tragedy, gut wrenching twists and turns move you through more and more adversity, and then ends with everyone home safely. That is how *all* really great stories play out. At least the ones they make movies about that I watch. I don't think I have ever paid money to go see a movie where the good guy dies and evil triumphs over good. That would be rather insidious. *Well there was that Simpson's movie… so I guess I am not 100% right.*

In the Apollo 13 movie they make reference to another Apollo launch that failed… the astronauts all died in a fire. I can't even remember which number that one was. Maybe it is because I didn't see a movie about that one. *Why?* Because it was never made. This one was because it is a classic story of success being birthed from impossible odds. That is what makes a truly great movie. I want to leave a legacy. I want my life, my family, my ministry, my marriage to end like that. I want my life to play out with *great success* coming out of *great adversity*. Can I close by challenging you to live up to this challenge? I challenge you to be the one who will say "This marriage will not die on my

91

watch!" I challenge you to look at the "nay" sayers and reply with, "Pardon me... but I believe this will be our finest hour!" Why will you say that? Because too much is *riding on it* to fail. There are too many watching. There are too many effected by your win, or your loss. Don't settle for your life being as a forgotten wind.

Live in such a way that you would not be ashamed to sell your parrot to the town gossip. –Will Rogers

Only those who overcome the odds go into the history books. Have you ever head of Harold Franklin Blithe? No... you haven't. Harold never did anything worthy of remembering. *I don't even know if I am spelling his name right, and his google search has come up blank.* That is a great shame. He could have left a legacy. Will you leave a legacy? Live a life that is truly worthy of a statue, or at least a well remembered impact on your children for the good.

A man is rich in proportion to the things he can afford to let alone. –Henry David Thoreau

The funeral I mentioned took over two hours. Why? There were many good things to say and many people who wanted to remember those things. This dear gentleman had started a mission that feeds over 8000 children every day in the Dominican Republic and in Haiti. His work continues on today and will continue on tomorrow. He left a legacy. He battled innumerable odds... fought thieves, battled malaria and dengue fever many times, took on voodoo priests, dug wells where there was no water, and the earth sprung forth. His life impacted mine, and the world will continue to be a better place because he decided not to follow the current of modern culture or a life of ease. He is one of my heroes!

A hundred times a day I remind myself that my inner and outer lives are based on the labors of other people, living and dead, and that I must exert myself in order to give in the same measure as I have received and am still receiving. –Albert Einstein

You can be a hero too... if in nothing more than your marriage. Your diligence... in your marriage... can leave a mark that will be remembered. It comes down to a question. *Do you have what it takes?* I believe you do. *I believe in you.* If it can happen for me it can happen for you. Maybe the real question has more to do with *will* you do what needs to be done? Leave a legacy. Please leave a legacy. I hope to sit down with you one day on the other side of this life and hear about your successful journey. *Until then...*

3.0

CEREMONIES OF UNITY

I believe in ceremonies. That which is not marked by ceremony is often forgotten. That which is marked by ceremony is remembered for years to come... maybe even lifetimes. I want to encourage you to bring ceremony to your commitments of change. Bare them before witnesses. Celebrate the newness with honor and expense. Make a big deal of this new life. Plan a full blown party! Bring out the champagne (if your not Baptist). Make your commitment to a new life with one another to be important beyond belief. I have included four ceremonial readings for you to use as you like. You may chose to write your own words. Two are for married couples and two are for singles. Of course you will want to use the appropriate one, your guests might not understand the humor of that mistake... but I would. Beyond the witnesses, these simple ceremonial confessions will allow you to make lifelong commitments to each other. These commitments lived out... will make your marriage great.

3.1

QUESTIONS AND RESPONSES FROM THE SEMINAR

The world in which we live is rather messy, yet there is joy in the journey if we want it bad enough to seek it with all of our hearts. A purpose filled life is found in getting in amongst the mess and helping another out. This is the essence of what it means to be truly human yet empowered by the Divine.

The following are a sampling of questions we have received at the marriage conferences, and the answers Terica or myself have given. I hope that these will possibly answer for you some of the questions that you may have. It is my hope that you can learn from these something the book may have missed. Now understand that these came in written form and the answers were given within the context of an adult only seminar. We do often invite singles to the events. They certainly need this information too, but everyone in the room is college age and older. The questions we get at the seminars tell us that there is a lot of hurt out there in this area, hurt that needs to be healed.

The significant problems we face cannot be resolved at the same level of thinking we were at when we created them. –Albert Einstein

The openness of many of these could never be voiced into a live microphone. Some of these are very blatant. These are real questions and real issues in which we are dealing with. I am just trying to keep it real and drag a few people back to the missed bases so they can win the game. *These questions are in no particular order… for this chapter was an afterthought and we had a publishing deadline to compete with!*

Q. Well I have had so many failed attempts at relationships. I have to admit I have gone way too far with most of them. I don't know if I can ever really have a good bond now. Is there any hope?

R. Yes, there is hope. With the help of the God that restores minds there is always hope. The God who can raise the dead can restore the mind. You must garner the courage to begin the process of healing. I suggest starting today on a fast of all media. This seems outrageous to the average person. Let me ask you a question. Would you tell a drug addict to just cut back on the crack a little until you can quit all together? I think not. You need a full separation from the negatively influencing stimuli. Singles should call a moratorium on dating. Set a time of one year before you will consider it. Set a time now and don't break it no matter how healed you think you are. This will be healthy for you. You can do it. Others have and not died. Well actually three died. Just joking. Nobody ever died from not being in a relationship. A lot of people have died from being in one. Start the restoration process now! Give God the time it takes to renew your mind. I suggest that you use this time to become a Biblical scholar.

Q. What is the biggest problem in marriages today?

R. Well I would bet that the secular experts would say "money" or at least some derivative of it. The fact that most americans are living way above there means certainly creates a series of friction points in a marriage. But I think that money is only the catalyst for a much deeper problem. I do know that the ability to handle money finds its way into many a young marriage, but it does that because we are basically selfish people who have not yet learned to live as one. Money is just an easy way to quantify, or should I say, prove on paper that one is taking more from a marriage than the other. Two people will quit fighting over money when they treat every dollar as a dollar that belongs to a very real God. When a couple becomes a genuine steward of the money they are allowed to handle, they will fight less over money, because it won't be their money to fight over. So in reality, our problems, big and small, all come from our inner self. When we are whole, we can become wholly integrated into another person. When we are broken, we cannot, and we will try to kill the other person getting them to fit into our broken mold.

Q. Why can't we just let the past be in the past and go on from here into the future? If God has forgiven us, who can stand in judgement against us?

R. Yes, from the perspective of time-lines the past is certainly the past. I can burn my house down today, and tomorrow I can go on as if nothing happened. But that would not be productive. That would be denial. I may have destroyed things in that house that belonged to to other people. Amends need to be made before the past can become the past. Until I have righted my personal wrongs I have no future, I am locked into an eternal today. The past is important because it impacts your future. We all need to deal with our past, and put it behind us properly. But never put the past behind you until you have dealt with it thoroughly and discovered every lesson that you could have possibly learned from it. Never leave the past to the past if there are still unresolved anger issues resulting from the memories of said past. That only leads to repeating the pain again and again. A great teacher once said, "Those who cannot remember the past are forced to repeat it." I personally believe that you will only find healing from the past when you are able to look back on any past situation and articulate what God has taught you through that circumstance, that it may be used to help another person through a similar circumstance, and thus bring glory to God because of it. Yes, even if that circumstance was one of great pain. The chief purpose of me is to bring glory to God, and then comes all the benefits for me! The old medicine commercial touted, "I haven't got time for the pain." I beg to differ! You haven't got time [not] to fully embrace, and [fully] exegete the pains of your past. Figure out your past and I can rightfully protect your future.

Q. What happens when my spouse and I cannot reach an agreement and we have to settle for a win-lose situation? Shouldn't the Man be in charge and have the final word?

R. I will answer the first part and let your Pastor handle the second part of your question! First off all we need to realize that in a marriage there is no win-lose situations. There is either win-win or lose-lose. When you are one, and biblically you are… if he loses… you lose! If she loses… you lose. When you are fighting for a marriage instead of against it, you are quick to realize that disagreements take on a different feel. When I am ticked off at Terica I tend to go for the jugular vein, and I know how to hit it. If I will stop long enough to focus on the fact that my wife is NOT the problem, only the delivery vehicle for what I estimate to be a problem, it puts my verbiage and attitude on a different pattern. Most fights are really over the inconsequential anyway. I watched on FOX News this morning a story about a Cambodian couple who split their house top to bottom with a chainsaw. That must have been some big fight! You should have seen the picture. It was pathetic. I'll bet it started over something like the removal of the garbage, her hair in the shower, his underwear on the floor, or her mother! I don't know. I do know that we need to be Men and Women who are wise enough to recognize when the enemy of our marriage is leading us by the nose into an argument over the inconsequential. Before you fight over anything, ask yourself the question, "Is this something I would want to die over?" Most marriages die over the inconsequential. We strain at a flea and swallow a camel.

Q. How can I learn to love my spouse again? You do not know what they have put me through.

R. I wish I had more information regarding this question. I am going to venture a guess that something has come between you that has hurt you, maybe hurt you both, and obviously hurt you badly. Remember that where there is God there is forgiveness. Now forgiveness does not mean that there is instantaneous forgetting. God has that forgetting ability, but we don't. Coming to a place of forgiveness is as good for you as it is for them. I suggest that you both go back and start the bonding process all over again. Date. Rekindle the early interests. Dedicate yourself to restoration. Fight the enemy that constantly reminds you of the point of pain. Replace it with memories of failures and consequential forgiveness you have received from God Himself.

Q. My Husband likes to watch pornographic material before and sometimes while we make love and that bothers me. What should I do?

R. Shoot him! No… I'm just kidding. Do you have a paring knife? First of all I need to address the phrase "make Love." Let's not refer to sex as "making love." It is what has been confusing the kids for a long time. It is sex! Great sex. Hot sex. Pleasure filled sex. But… it is sexual intercourse. *Making Love* is better described as the mutual combining of the four types of Love to form a bonded love. Now about the pornography. Ouch! Here is a person, I say person because It doesn't say if it is a Man or Woman, but from the handwriting I would say it was about a Man. Here is a Man who is most likely unable to be aroused unless they are stimulated to some hyper degree. The unfortunate result of watching porn for so long is that the primary victim (and as you can see both parties are actually victims in this case) of this is no longer able to have a healthy sexually stimulating relationship with a real person. This is sad and tragic. This is robbing both partners the ability to have the intimacy that they were designed to have. See your spouse as a victim also. Though it hurts you horribly, he is a victim too. This person needs help. There are support groups for those addicted to porn. Find one. This act is a perverting of the bond at least, and most likely what could be defined as adultery. Have you talked to him about it? Don't talk to him at the time of the act. Make an appointment to share how it makes you feel. Don't browbeat him. Just simply share how it makes you feel. I would hope this person can see the hurt they are causing their spouse and seek forgiveness and restoration of their mind for the sake of the marriage. This person needs to go back through the restorative process and get healthy enough to have sex. Right now they are obviously not. Find a good male counselor that you can both trust to openly deal with this. I say "male" because he will most likely hear this truth from another Man he respects than from a female.

Q. I get so mad sometimes and say things I should not. What can I do to help?

R. My mother used to tell me to count to ten. With a mouth like mine, ten seconds only allowed me to more fully articulate my anger in words and cutting remarks that would hurt worse. I know that some counselors will tell you not to let yourself bury an point of friction because it will only come up again. That is right and wrong. It is right that you should not bury a point of friction between you, but you should schedule a calmer time to articulate your difference. This delay is much better that delivering a verbal death blow to your spouse for something that really matters little. If you are one of these [anger] people, and you know who you are, take a time out. Go articulate your words on paper. Writing my anger tends to slow me down because I don't write as fast as I can spew sarcasm's. Don't use a word processor either! One guy at a seminar reminded me that his wife could type at 80+ words a minute. If you are one of those fast fingered typists, I suggest that you utilize a notebook and a dull pencil and write long hand in block letters. Heck, use a calligraphy pen if you need to, but put a little time between you and a disagreement. I know that the bible says that we should not let the sun go down on our wrath. So don't. Give no place for wrath to begin with. Wrath is an asinine action for a human anyway. God is the only one allowed to legitimately have wrath. So let us dispel that misquote right out of the box. But if I might add… this verse was written when people went to bed at sunset. They did not have lights, which allowed them to be up late, and thus irritate each other later, thus fight later. So if you get into a disagreement after the sun has already gone down, wait until tomorrow to discuss it, the sun will have not gone down because it already did. Take a little time, alone, and seek to discover if the issue is really worth even bringing up again, or if the issue at hand is actually what you are upset about. Often I find myself saying in the morning, "Honey… remember last night? It really doesn't matter. If you think your mother needs to move in with us… I am fine with that… and certainly I would welcome all twelve of her cats." The last part of that was both sarcastic and untrue… she only has six cats.

Q. I am afraid to talk to my spouse about what I am feeling?

R. Wow, I wish I had more to go on here. Let me just wallow out some ideas. First off, spouses, you need to be a person who articulates to your spouse, "There is no hurt in your world that I do not want to bare with you." This goes for the Men and Women both. Your spouse needs to find you a safe and loving ear. I personally have to rush going into fix-it mode. I am a fixer! "Well let me make a call!" "I'll get on the phone and tell them a thing or two…" As a spouse I need to let my beloved one articulate her pain, and just share it for a while. Jesus was touched with the feelings of our infirmities (Hebrews 4:15). If we are to be like Him, and let me say that He would have made a great spouse, we need to allow ourselves to embrace the pain.

Q. My spouse likes to participate in positions and situations that I am not comfortable in? Are there lines that need to be drawn in this area?

R. I will venture to think I understand exactly what you are talking about. Unfortunately most Men (and some Women) have been so impacted by the sexual mis-information of the perverted media that there minds have come to believe they are missing something unless they have "this" type, or "that" type of sex. There are multiple books on positions, and styles. Let me speak to the Men here very boldly. I am all for creativity… but… I want to encourage all spouses to major on face to face moments. Magically honest moments that allow you to expend your physical experience looking into each others eyes. What could be more awesome and holy as to look into the window of another persons soul, while being fully exposed (naked) to each other and yet fully and completely accepted? To view the spark in each others eye as you experience a pleasure that is reserved for none other? If you want to limit your experience with your spouse as nothing more than an available sexual provider you can… but you are missing out on what can be awesomely reciprocal and not just physically receptacle. I know that Olivia encouraged us to "Let's get animal!" It does not take long to find out that is really not what we are looking for? Adam was given that option. He declined. You are supposed to be in love, and not in heat. Treat your spouse like a beloved human being and not like a mounted mare. Could it be a trick of the enemy to keep us from looking into the soul of our beloved?

Q. My husband is very jealous… what can I do to fix that?

R. May I ask what you are doing, or that he thinks you are doing that makes him jealous? It may be schizophrenia… but it may actually be founded in something real. If there is something that he finds unacceptable… stop doing it. Isn't the main responsibility of the spouse to please the other, and vice versa? The Man for the Woman and the Woman for the Man! Honor your spouse as Christ loved the Church and gave Himself for it. Christ is the example. If we are a Christ follower then we will do the same. Shouldn't he be expected to change also? Yes, but it seems like you are wanting to know what to do right now and not him. So we always start where we can. With us first.

Q. My husband likes to role play during our intimate times. I am uncomfortable with that. What should I do?

R. I am venturing a guess that you are talking about dressing up, and or pretending to be someone you are not. Let me speak to the spouses (male or female) here a minute. Love the one your with! The Scantily dressed naughty nurse didn't marry you. Her time came at a price of 3.95 a minute! I would find it rather insulting if my wife asked me to let her call me Bruce Willis. Now admittedly I do like to dress up like Superman from time to time… but not to get hooked up with Louis Lane. I just like wearing a cape and my underwear on the outside of my spandex leotards. Sorry… just joking. Please realize that most of our desire to role play comes from foreign stimuli… pornography. That is wrong. It is adultery. It perverts the bond and pollutes the relationship. Don't insult your spouse. Get help. I want to encourage everyone to fantasize about the one who actually loves you back.

Q. How can you expect a man to be completely unstained by what is around him?

R. I can't! I don't! I won't! We have all been stained by this world. I can however expect that after a person sincerely desires to be a totally devoted follower of Christ that he or she will take all steps necessary from that point on to keep themselves wholly true for their holy significant other. I realize that you may be watching *The Andy Griffith Show* and on will come the *Victoria Secret Sluts*. What is a real Man to do? Well you could look away. Some of you Men and Women are calling me gay. Shame on you. I call myself a lover who is saving my mind for my beloved. Will we always be able to negotiate our eyes away from perversion? No, but can we make a concerted effort to not look twice, or three times, or four? Yes. I know that to be true.

Q. I grew up with pornography. Is there any help for me?

R. No! You are going to be a pervert… get used to it! Not really. *That was sarcasm!* Of course there is help and wholeness for you. If Jesus can raise people from their death bed, He can certainly raise people from their bed of iniquity. Praise the Lord that there is restoration of the mind. Praise the Lord that there is the washing of regeneration. Work through the steps to restore your mind as you would restoring a bond. Don't wait until you are married. Don't wait until it raises its ugly head in your face. Begin refilling your mind with the pure Word of God and the bad stuff will have to run from your mind. Eat the good - and force out the bad. Make a vow to cut it off now... and go from here different. Make a renewed commitment every day to live pure. Because it matters! It matters to your spouse, it matters to your children, it matters to your children's children. This is important stuff here... eternally important.

Q. I'm married to a person who is not right for me. What should I do?

R. Let's take this a step at a time. More than likely you are in this relationship because you became joined when neither of you were whole. If you were completely whole yourself, you wouldn't have jumped into this. So you must show the same grace that you have been given. It is tough. Unfortunately it may get tougher. Certainly you could say, "This person is adulterating our marriage" and walk out. That would not be right. I believe that to walk out on any marriage (even an adulterous situation) without first exhausting all the efforts to save it is dead wrong. First of all you need to begin a quest to find personal wholeness. Then and only then will you be able to see clearly what needs to be done. You think your whole now? Great! Get *whole-er*! I know that isn't a recognized word... but recognize it for us today. Okay? Then find a godly professional counselor to help you make decisions regarding the steps you need to take to first bring your spouse to wholeness. Remember that whether or not you were whole at the time, you signed a contract of *Agape* and you stood before witnesses and promised *Storge*. Work with that counselor to devise a plan to bring restoration and conversion to your spouse. Do not rush into the divorce clause without having first been the consummate definition of grace and restoration.

Q. I am dating a person who is not right for me. How do I get out of this?

R. Have you ever walked out of a movie because it wasn't any good? Get up and walk out. Do it now! Be mature and tell them face to face in a public place. Then say, "Excuse me I need to powder my nose," and keep on walking. If you are a Man, the powder my nose should get them to walk out. Call it off. You most likely hear begging and promises. Ignore them! You do not want a person to change for you. You want a whole person who is whole for themselves so they can be whole for you. Did that make sense? I want to be a whole person because God called me to that. Then and only then can I be whole for another person.

Q. I am not a big talker. I don't talk a lot to anyone. How can I learn to communicate with my wife?

R. I am not a big talker either. This is a good question for Men and Women. Simply learn to ask questions and listen. "Tell me more? How did that make you feel? How do you think they felt about that? Do you think that was a good idea? What would you have done in that situation? If you could do it again what would you do differently?" Listen to what your spouse is saying. I'll bet these six questions would keep you in conversation all night and you would find that [if you really listen to the answers] your spouse will come to think of you as a tremendous communicator. You might even get a bonus question!

Q. My husband thinks that sex is a two minute affair. What should I tell him?

R. Well first of all be thankful that he is able to reach his potential with you in that alloted time. You must know how to please him. On a more serious note, remind him that you are designed differently that he is. He peaked sexually at eighteen years old, you peaked already or will peak in your mid-thirties. Does not that alone tell you that Mars and Venus work on different time tables? Two minutes is said to be average for a Man. No Man wants to be average. I want to challenge the Men who are reading this to be above average. I challenge you to outlast her! We like challenges. Remember that your dear Wife is turned on by what you say and do all day. The way you treat her at the breakfast table will move the evening along much quicker for her... and thus for you. The kind words you whisper in her ear at supper, or during the movie, or even the game, will help you to find a common timing later in the evening. Tell him you want more of him. Talk to him honestly about this. Men have greater control in this area than they let on to have. *Sorry guys... I had to tell the truth!*

Q. My wife thinks that sex once every two weeks is more than enough to satisfy me? Its not. How do I tell her?

R. It's the Thursday night is our night question! Okay... here's the secret. Sit down and say, "Honey, I want to experience your intimate love on a more regular basis. You drive me wild. You excite me! I need you more than you could ever know." Now was that so hard? I think not. Most Women will respond very favorably if they understand that you want them, and not just sex. Make sure that your experiences are keeping her emotional needs in mind as well as your physical needs. If your times together are quality times for her, you might find her more willing to participate on a more regular basis. Wives... listen... don't send your husband out into the overtly sexually supercharged world frustrated. This is asking for trouble. This can cause a good Man to become adulterous. Your denial can be the root cause of the a major crash to come.

Q. I can't keep from looking at other Women? What should I do?

R. Poke your eye out. I'll bet that will stop the problem! Of course you could always get some scissors and go to cutting in another area if you need to not be blind to keep your job. This goes the same for Women too. Seriously... get some help. Find another Man who will be your accountability partner on this. My friend and great comedian, I will call him Tom to protect his anonymity, spoke to a group of Comedians at a retreat we had a few years ago. He spoke of his own past battle in this area. This awesomely talented Man gave his personal cell phone number out to the entire group and made us an amazing offer. He said, "If you ever find yourself struggling in a hotel room to remain pure... call me... whatever time it is... and I will help talk you through it." He went on to address the serious consequences of this matter. Find an accountability partner like that! Find someone who will call you every day. Find someone who will watch your schedule and call you when you are on the road and in a strange hotel room. *No I will not give you Tom's telephone number... his phone is probably ringing off the hook right now from those guys alone.* Take steps everyday to do better. Pray often. Do you ask God for the strength to be pure every day? Do that! Prayer changes things. *I know that because there is a bumper sticker that says that!* Fill your mind with good stuff and don't feed the lustful desires. The old Man dies a hard death - but he does die. As good old St. Francis says, "It is in dying that we are born to eternal life." *Well I think it was St. Francis... it could have been another bumper sticker. I have found it to be true no the less.*

3.2

FOR ADDITIONAL STUDY

There are so many verses that pertain to our topic that are not listed in this book. I suggest you do your own search of the Bible to find out more information in which to design your life by. We have included them as reference point for those who are doing further investigation of this topic. *Memorize these verses and the ones in the book and you will be a virtual marital theologian.* So get out your own Bible and look them up. The Bible is a wonderful Holy book that offers clarity and answers for our life.

Genesis 38:9	Matthew 19:4-5	1 Corinthians 7:33-34
Deuteronomy 22:22	Matthew 19:9	1 Corinthians 7:39
Deuteronomy 22:13-20	Matthew 19:18	1 Corinthians 9:27
Deuteronomy 22: 20-27	Mark 10:11-12	1 Corinthians 10:8
Deuteronomy. 24:1	Mark 10:19	1 Thessalonians 4:3
Proverbs 6:26	Luke 16:18	1 Thessalonians 5:22
Proverbs 6:32	Luke 18:20	Galatians 5:19
Leviticus 20:10	John 8:3-4	Galatians 5:19
Leviticus 20:10	Romans 1:29	Ephesians 5:3
Job 24:15	Romans 2:22	Ephesians. 5:22-25
Isaiah 57:3	Romans 7:3-4	James 2:11
Jeremiah 3:8	Romans 13:9	1 Peter 3:7
Ezekiel 16:32	1 Corinthians 5:1	2 Peter 2:14
Matthew 5:32	1 Corinthians 5:11	Hebrews 12:16
Matthew 5:28	1 Corinthians 6:13-18	Hebrews 13:4
Matthew 7:3	1 Corinthians 6:18-20	Hebrews 13:9
Matthew 19:4-6	1 Corinthians 7:2	Jude 1:7
Matthew 19:9	1 Corinthians 7:10	

4.0

A SHORT VERSION OF THE ENTIRE BOOK

Never Buy A Man Reading Lamp That Wont Fit In His Bathroom

While sitting on the airplane on my way to do one of our seminars last week I saw an ad from a company that condenses the world's greatest business books into an easy to read 8 page synopsis of the book. What a great idea! I would be a reader if every book was 8 pages long. I'll bet my book shelf would be full of those. *Just think, the whole collection could fit on the top of my toilet… for reference of course.* I might actually read two or even three books a year that way. So with that thought in mind, I have prepared this short version of the entire book for those who don't have the time to read the entire book or for those who are not sure you want to invest the time to read this book. I simply sat down and tried to sum up what I wrote in the last two-hundred and thirty un-edited pages. Maybe I should have done that to begin with and it wouldn't have taken us five years to complete. Then again, the publisher couldn't charge 16.99 for an ten page coloring book either. A lot of good stuff had to be skipped… because that is the only way I could get it down to a bathroom reader size. Nevertheless, I hope this incomplete synopsis that is filled with sweeping generalities and random thoughts will encourage you to go back and read the entire book. Here we go:

MEN MOVED TO MARS WHEN WOMEN STARTED KILLING THE ONES ON VENUS

Quid pro quo! Can you really have a great marriage? Yes you can have a great marriage! There I said it! It can be achieved. The mediocrity myth is over. The truth is out. The cover has been blown. The banner has been lifted. The white smoke has come from the papal chimney! *Okay that last one didn't make any sense, sorry!* Without a doubt we know that there are people… on this planet… many… who have great marriages. So it is doable. It is achievable.

Puppy love leads to a dog's life, but it's real to the puppy. –Bob Harrington

The problem is achieving it. Anyone who has tried it knows it is not that simple. How do you blend two people groups who seem to be from totally different planets? Mars Men and Venus Women are very-very, very-very different. *You don't have to be a rocket scientist or subscribe to National Geographic to understand that.* By the time you are seven years old you have come to that basic understanding. Of course the differences go way beyond what meets the eye. One might venture to say that these two people groups use the same words… but speak a different language. On the other hand, Men and Women have some great similarities. Throwing caution to the wind, Men and

Women continue to discover that they bring to each other something they both need desperately. *Oneness from two!*

Men and Women belong to different species, and communication between them is still in its infancy.

Now with Man and Woman now sharing the same space there have been some pretty interesting conflicts that have arisen. Each has attempted to make their new home on Earth more to their personal liking. So Woman, in her wisdom has attempted to tame this wild animal known as Man. The observant Woman has found that at best a wild Man can only be trained… but never tamed. Conversely Man has tried with all of his might to shrug off any training and remain the hunter-gatherer and king of his jungle, albeit the jungle is now made of concrete, tile, and wall to wall carpeting. Man likes the invention of indoor toilets, but that may be as far as it goes. Contemporary Man has conversely tried to *en-wild* Womankind only to realize that the process has somehow reduced the attraction he had to her in the first place. These challenges have caused some to fight, some to rebel, and some to give up on love altogether. That is a crying shame. In the next few pages I will show you where it all went wrong and how to fix it. Yes that is a mighty big promise. *That's just the way I roll!*

If Women didn't exist all the money in the world would have no meaning. –Multi-millionaire Aristotle Onassis

For some of you singles reading this book you may think it is just for marrieds. WRONG! Married people may read the first part of this synopsis and think it is just for singles. WRONG! That is just what the enemy of your relationships wants you to think. I challenge you to look at my (proven) hypothesis and see if you don't agree with it. It basically goes like this: Most marriages and relationships in general have problems because they are built on a faulty foundation! There, that was simple. Like dilapidated house, if you go back and fix the foundation, then and only then can you fix the house and get the walls to square and the floors to level. *Please pardon the construction illustration but I feel like it is mostly Men who are reading this version of the book… so get over it.* So it is all about foundation! The problems you are having in achieving a great marriage (or a great pre-marital relationship), is a matter of going back and re-pouring a proper foundation.

I married her for her looks… but not the looks she's been giving me lately!

So what is this foundation? You may be thinking that this is where the author tries to insert his brand of "salvation" or "religious experience" into the book in secret hopes that the reader will become his brand of "religious" person? Wrong! Rather what I am going to share with you, though founded in Biblical truth, is universal truth. Whether you are a Protestant or a Catholic, a religious fanatic or a reprobate, truth is always truth. Like gravity, truth is truth for every race, creed, and certainly sex on this planet. That truth is that great marriages come from great bonds between average people.

It's rough being a Man. See, Men have to have money, have to try to look good, have to have the right job, the right prestige; Women can be working in McDonald's—we'll still try to get your phone number. –Sinbad

A great bond is like an *epoxy glue*. *J B Weld is my personal favorite!* Epoxy glue is different from the *Elmers* paste we used to eat as a child, or the *Testors model* glue that was dangerously intoxicating as we built plastic cars and airplanes on the kitchen table as young boys. An *epoxy* is strengthened not by it's exposure to air, rather by the combining of multiple ingredients, from multiple tubes. After all the ingredients are mixed, there is usually a very short set up time, but then… BAM… it is solid as a rock. Like the *epoxy* glue, there are four key ingredients that need to go into your great bond and subsequent great marriage. These four ingredients when combined in equal proportions will form a lifelong bonded love and become the basis for a happy lifelong partnership. If either party leaves any of these ingredients out of their foundation they are dooming their relationship to trouble. There is hope! Don't be discouraged. Foundations can be rebuilt. Do you ever watch HGTV? Then you know it can be done… for houses… and relationships.

These four ingredients would have formed naturally if Man and Woman had not been so jaded by a sexually perverse media. This did not happen overnight. For years the secular media has taught us that "making love" is sex. When it is not really sex at all. Sex is sex! It is good, it is great, hot sex, awesome sex, it is glorious and sensual, it is pleasure-filled… but it is sex. Sex in itself does not make a good marriage. I'll bet you already knew that. *Because most of us are closet geniuses.* So let us move on.

Women color their hair, apply make-up, purchase a wonder bra and a booty enhancing girdle… and have the audacity to claim to be only looking for a Man who will love them for who they really are.

Before I define the bonding ingredients let me tell you about *Velcro* love. Because it is the popular option these days. We all love *Velcro*. *Velcro* is a glorious connective cloth that allows you to instantly hook up two different items. After a few years of connecting and disconnecting the ability of the *Velcro* to hold securely is rather weak. In fact it is almost non-existent. This unfortunately is the kind of relationships that modern society has been propagating. You have been taught their version of *Velcro* love since you were old enough to understand the birds and the bees. Nevertheless it has failed miserably and the bodies are strewn by the hi-way in the wake of this dung. Do you want to make your relationship solid? Do you want to make your marriage great? I hope you do.

I wanted to marry her from the first moment I saw the moonlight shining on the barrel of her father's shotgun. –Rich Praytor

All four of these ingredients are almost one and the same.. in a way. For what makes a great marriage is love. Not just any love, but the four different types of love congealed together. Did you know there were four types? Well there are. I am going to share them along with a simple way of remembering them. *There is nothing like a good acrostic to jog the memory.*

L.O.V.E.

L — Look At That!

Eros is a love type that can best be described as adoration. It is that quickening of the mind, the pitter-patter of the heart, that uncontrollable infatuation that one has when they see that special someone. It happens in a moment. Boom… there they are. It is lived out in adoration. You can't keep your eyes off of them. Everything about them intrigues you. You are enamored. I would call it worship. I call it that because it is the same feeling we express as we sing songs of adoration to our God. When you are in the throes of *Eros* you are blind to everything else. This is a must have ingredient in a great bond… and subsequent great marriage. For our discussion, *Eros* is summed up in the statement: *Look at that!* Do you… or did you have this?

When we first met my wife didn't like me that much. Luckily, she wanted to stay in this country. –Brian Kiley

O — Our Commonality

Philia is a love type that is best described as common fellowship and shared interest. It is the commonality you find with another in things you like to do, hobbies, activities, dreams you share, and adventures you take together. It is friendship love. Don't let that scare you. If you are going to have a great marriage you are going to have to at least be great friends with your spouse. Without that you are merely sleeping with the enemy. This is where the basis for lifelong mutual interest will keep you united in your conversation for a lifetime. Without it there will be little to talk about other than the kids… and that *aint* enough to make a relationship great. Trust me on this one. For our discussion *Philia* will be summed up in what I call: *Our Commonality*. Do you… or did you have this?

Those who love deeply never grow old; they may die of old age, but they die young. –A.W. Pinero

V — Vulnerably Safe

Storge is a love type best described as trust love. It is revealed as we reach the point in a relationship that we share the innermost desires and fears of our hearts. It develops as we feel safe enough to reveal the flaws in our self without the fear of rejection. *Storge* doesn't come overnight. It can't be achieved until the first two love types are well developed. This is the most often overlooked type of love. Without it, your marriage is doomed to divorce as time plays its nasty tricks on our bodies and health. I often refer to this as the love type that allows a spouse to sit for hours holding the hand of their beloved in the often tragic golden years of a relationship. This is the love that says, "Don't worry… you wont die alone." Please go back and read the illustration in the full book to get a better understanding of this. For our discussion we will simply consider *Storge* under the heading: *Vulnerably Safe*. Do you… or did you have this?

I was a fool to have married my wife, but she was so infatuated with me she didn't seem to notice. –Emo Philips

E — Everlasting Promise

Agape is a love type that could be best described as a everlasting promise. Covenant love! Now we live in an age where contracts are made to be broken. Or at least that is what the attorney's would have us to believe. *Agape* love is a heart given promise to love until death do we part. It is a signed contract promising to our spouse that we will give ourselves exclusively unto them, mind, body, and emotions. *No asterisks!* It is witnessed best in the marriage ceremony and lived out best in a lifelong commitment to each other. It is often referred to as the God type love. It is a choosing to love eternally. For our discussion and for our ability to remember it, we will call it: *Everlasting Promise*. Do you… or did you have this?

All you need is love!

Yes… all you need is *love* to have a great marriage. Unfortunately many, if not most people enter into marriage without having all of the key ingredients of real love. They may have the *Look at that - infatuation factor* going on, they may have even chosen to get legally married, but without *all four love ingredients* solidly in place, their bonding glue will never dry. Their marriage cannot last. Some overtly spiritual people might say that all we need is *Agape* love. They say, "If it is good enough for God it should be all we need." It only takes a few minutes of good searching the *Bible* and *real life* to find out that these people have been out in the sun to long and have never read the *Song of Solomon*. You need all of these love types to secure lifelong happiness in marriage. All of these love ingredients are designed to gel and harden into an awesome love that is culminated in a great marriage and a totally awesome sex life too.

Now this teaching comes with an interesting little catch. Every one of these love types ingredients) bring to the marriage table a different marriage-long quality along with them. To miss any along the way is to miss the fullness of a great marriage and miss the awesomeness of a great bond. Hear these next sentences very well. *The percentage of time one spends in each of these four quadrants of love will determine the percentage of time spent in that quadrant during marriage. Many people skip through the types of love so fast they do not allow that quadrant to really take hold and stir together in their life.* Secular media has told us to have *Eros*… and get into bed… quickly. Societal norms have told us to *get it on* with our friends. The teens call it, "Friends with benefits." They teach us to find someone we enjoy being around and share mutual sexual plea-sures the way you would share a round of golf. Keep on playing it that way and you could eventually loose all your golf equipment! *Storge* love is all but written off in our self-serving narcissistic world. There are going to be a lot of lonely seniors in the days to come. As far as lifelong commitments go… culture has taught us to keep our options open. *Who needs Agape? We change our minds more often than we change our underwear.* I think that last line would make a great bumper sticker!

This skipping of, and/or rapidly rushing through any of these steps impedes our ability to really love and be fully loved. Skip the adoration time and you will find yourself not even attracted to your spouse about the middle of your first marital year. You will ques-tion what you saw in them in the first place. *Was I drunk? I don't even drink. I must have been drugged or something.* You will start looking at others. Skip the commonality portion and you will find that you have nothing in common, and thus have nothing to talk about. I would hate to spend the rest of my life with someone to whom I had nothing to say. Skip the trust building vulnerability step and you will live in fear of getting old, getting ill, or being honest and vulnerable with your spouse. We all need at least one person we can be totally vulnerable with… and that really needs to be the one who is always going to be there for us. Skip the Covenant (marriage contract) and you have nothing to keep you in the same room, much less the same house when you are having a bad day. Troubled times come… genuine covenant keeps you working for change instead of calling a moving van or having an affair.

Many of you may be rightfully saying that you are already married and cannot undo the missing steps you have taken. Wrong! No matter where you are you can go back to the first base and start again. It may take a little more time than it would have if you had done it right the first time. It can be done.

Men think that Women like Men who are dangerous. As a result Men smoke, drink, and ride a motorcycle without a helmet. The reality… Women don't like guys who are dangerous. They want us to think that because they are trying to kill us. –Dennis Miller

Do you have a relationship with all of these types of love fully in place and working well? If not, you need to start the restoration process today. Only put off for tomorrow the things that don't matter. This is the most important thing on your horizon right now. Fix it. Fix it now. How do we do that? Well if you will send me a check for $29.95 I will send you a little bottle of pills! *LOL!* Only you can fix the problem. You start the fixing in the following manner.

Restoration of the heart comes first with a deep and honest desire to *really* fix it. Sometimes the cost of the repair is quite high. Then again, the cost of leaving things the way they are is higher. The cost to children involved in the mix makes divorce virtually unfathomable. *Well at least I would hope you find it unfathomable.* Certainly it is easier to *cut our losses* and start again. As creatures of habit, you will most likely make the same mistake over and over again. So why not fix it now instead of waiting to fix it in the midst of your next failed attempt? You only have so many years… why waste them in repeated misery?

We are *all* broken beings. Until we realize that we've got some problems of our own we will never be able to have a great marriage. If you are waiting on your spouse to change and make you happy - get ready for some major lifelong disappointment. The key to having a great spouse starts with being a great spouse. You may think you are a great spouse already. *Sure… great… whatever.* Get over it! We have all got some issues. Before you can help get the cataract out of your spouses eye, you need to get a some new glasses yourself. *Lens Crafters - in about an hour!* You need to be a whole person or you will kill your spouse trying to make them bring peace and wholeness to your own life. It is time that you took responsibility for your own world. Can you admit that you have a few problems? If you said yes, read on. *If not, flush the toilet on this book and get a good lawyer.*

The healing process begins as we realize that we have personally made mistakes and being truly sorry for them. Let me make this personal. Be broken hearted enough about your own failures to let the repairs start with you. Do this whether your spouse comes along or not, your future healing and wholeness is at stake. Many people go into marriage thinking that *this* person will bring *that* missing element to *their* life. When they don't - they try and kill the other person trying to force them to bring happiness and peace to their own existence. It just wont happen. Miserable people will only become more miserable and make others miserable with them. So let's start our own healing by admitting that *we* have a problem. The problem is that we have sinned. We are, or at least we were in the past selfish-self-serving-sinners. We rushed through our bonding steps and became focused on ourselves, and our own desires, instead of doing what it really took to achieve a great marriage. Whether that be by ignorance or choice… we sinned, and we need to repent. So a thinking person would first want to make amends with the God who they sinned against… and the person they sinned against also. There are some great restorative techniques given in the larger book. Read them.

Married Men live longer than single Men…
But married Men are more willing to die!

While I'm here I need to mention something about sex. Understand that sex alone, good sex, great sex will not make up for any missing steps in your bonding experience. Understand that you can put all the gas you want into the car… but if the engine aint right… it aint gonna' run! Sex is good! I mention this because *some* people might think *some* Christian teachers are anti-sex. Especially if you are just reading this synopsis. No way. I am pro sex! I believe in it, love it, and enjoy it. But… sex is not "making love" by any shape of the imagination. The term *[making love]* has been totally perverted by the media. Sex is sex. God designed it. He implemented it. He smiles upon it within the confines of a fully bonded relationship. So don't hear [anti-sex] in any way. It is good. Participate as often as you can. It is healthy for you. Not only will it allow you to burn off that extra helping of mashed potatoes you had at supper, but studies show that if done often enough, will actually reduce the risk of certain types of cancer in Men. Within marital confines - get busy - get healthy. Look into the eyes of your spouse and share what God wants you to share. There is a book chapter that addresses the act of masturbation. *I could not condense it enough to include it in this mini-book, but it is rather ingenious… and a must read… I humbly say.*

How am I supposed to love my wife as Christ loved the church? I'm doing good just trying to keep myself from strangling her with my WWJD bracelet!

Here's a little trivia for you. Did you know that many cultures, including ancient biblical cultures required the couple to have sex before they were married? They did. They had to prove to each other and the Priest that would perform the ceremony that they were wholly bondable. The Priest felt that if someone had given themselves sexually to another they could not give themselves fully to the one they were betrothed to. *Scary!* You need to read this chapter in the book. There is not time in this synopsis, but it is a very interesting *page-turner* study!

Part Two

Once I was young and virtually indestructible and now I am an old married guy on a January morning on Sturgis Avenue in St. Paul sniffing the wind and taking my vitamins. Six a.m. It's pitch-black out. Fresh coffee in the air. I take vitamin C, E, B complex, Lysine, cod-liver oil, echinacea, with orange juice, which eases the pills down the gullet. I do forty leg stretches, forty crunches, twenty push-ups, a dozen curlies, on the living room floor. I don't want to struggle when I get out of the car. And if tonight my queen should reach over from her side of the bed and draw me to her, I intend to be capable of knighthood. –Garrison Keillor

I trust that you now understand a little about where we have failed in our attempts to be fully bonded, and are taking steps to go back and correct those mistakes. For now, how do we deal with the day to day problems that arise in marriage? *I have come to know that it aint easy living with an alien.* In many ways that is what the opposite sex is - an alien! It is going to take a little humility, compassion, and knowledge to live with another culture. You need a lot of give and a lot of take. Fortunately it can be done successfully. Fortunately you don't have to be a rocket scientist. I have met many a happily married couple who were dumber than a stump, and I have met a number of happily married couples whose I.Q.'s were off the charts. This is not about brains, it is about taking on the challenge of merging two interplanetary cultures. It is not for the lazy. So if you are lazy… stop being lazy.

My wife and I took out insurance policies on one another - so now it's just a waiting game. –Bill Dwyer

Understand that though we feel it would be great to have a spouse that thought and acted just like we do, it would be rather boring. Our attraction from the start was congealed in our differences. Women are soft and cuddly for the most part, and Men are wild at heart. Celebrate that difference. Ladies need to stop trying to fully domesticate the lion they married. Get him domesticated enough not to pee on the floor, but remember you love him for being a lion. Men need to stop trying to turn your delicate princess into a NASCAR lovin' Hooters girl. They may look really attractive carrying a bucket of wings… but we had our chance to bring *that kind* home to momma and we didn't… we didn't for a reason. Celebrate that reason. Celebrate what each of you bring to the marriage table.

No wonder my wife lost her mind; she's been giving me a piece of it every day for 20 years. –Nazareth

Men and Women speak different dialects. We use the same words but mean different things. When a Man says "frank" he is referring to a hot dog. When a Woman says "frank" she is referring to honest concise communication. A Woman will say, "Be honest… do these jeans make my butt look fat?" She is actually wanting to be reassured that you still love her body and that she looks thin. Every Man in the world knows that by the first year of his marriage. You understand. A citizen of Mexico could go to Spain and understand their language, but you wouldn't want that person to interpret a life altering medical document. Some of the words are understood differently. Their Spanish will have different tenses, and different different implications. It is no different with us. We need to listen closely to each other and become *bilingual* if we are going to have a foreigner living with us peacefully under the same roof.

I've heard that dogs are Man's best friend. That explains where they get their hygiene tips. –Kelly Maguire

Men have learned to trash talk from the time they could articulate an insult. They love it. Women have been learning etiquette and pomp since they were old enough to have tea parties with imaginary princesses. Men come home and start with their sarcastic office talk and Women get their feelings hurt. Women try and talk to Men with the daintiness of a doily and get ignored because their conversation is thought of in a Mans world as just shy of *effeminate!* If we are going to achieve a great marriage we must realize that the way we say things is as important to our spouse as what we say. This comes back to our need to be *bilingual*. Every year I go to the Dominican Republic to do mission and social work. I often threw things from the moving truck to people on the side of the road. Not because I didn't want to touch them. It was simply because somebody else was driving and I wanted to bless them with a bag of rice or a baseball for their kids as we passed them. My Dominican interpreter pulled me aside and told me that in his culture, to throw something to someone was a sort of insult, and came off as arrogant and uncaring. I certainly didn't intend to do that. So I had to learn to give in a way the Dominican people could receive. That way was hand to hand and face to face. So that is how I shared from that point on. I thought nothing of meeting their cultural expectations. Why? Because I wanted to let them know I care in a language they could understand. We need to do that for our spouses. *Do you get it?* It is pretty simple when you stop to think about it.

When I met Mr. Right I had no idea his first name was Always. –Rita Rudner

Women are givers and Men are takers. At least that is what I have been told. Truth is that Women are takers too. For the most part Men will be happy in letting the Woman give and give and give. *I'm cool with that!* This is done under the auspices that *Women are givers - so let them be who they are.* Well Woman are takers too, but they take in different ways. Women need to take from a spouse time, love, and adoration. This is *Eros* and *Storge* personified here. Maybe a little Philia thrown in for good measure as well. Little gifts to a Woman are like back massages to us. A simple card and flowers goes a long way in meeting this *taking* need for a female. Men like to take in other areas. *You figure out what those might be.* It is not the obvious! Men need that too, but they also need respect and appreciation for their hard work. They are hunter-gatherers who have been forced to go to work in a steel and glass enclosed box for you and the family. Give them the respect that gift deserves and you will see your marriage turn around.

If a Man finds a wife he has found a good thing – but if a Man finds a million dollars in small unmarked bills it would be better if keeps quiet about it.

Celebrate marriage! Scientist say that Married people enjoy a healthier life, and a more fulfilled sex life. Marriage is good for you. Every week you should bake a cake and sing *Happy Anniversary to Us.* Let the kids join in if you have them. *If not borrow some from a neighbor.* Marriage is a good thing. Marriage is a God thing. Men need to look at there wife with the same desire they did when they walked down the isle. This spouse is the Queen of your castle. Treat her that way. Make your children and/or step-children treat her that way also. Women need to treat the Men as the King of the castle. You too need to require your children to do this as well. Marriage is good for you. It doesn't always feel like it at times. Neither does eating an apple a day. *In the long run this is a great thing… it keeps those evil Doctors away.* Are you celebrating your marriage? Maybe you don't think you can right now. Well start by celebrating the *institution of marriage* and then let it move on to you in a personal way as you progress in achieving a great marriage.

The difference between Men and Women can be reduced to this; Women don't find farts amusing! –Justin Fennell

We all value what we bring to any situation differently. I happen to think I am worth at least fifty dollars an hour wherever I am working. Most of my bosses have felt differently. Those cheap… well you know. It is not that different in any relationship including our marriage. I am not saying that it is right, just that it is. A Man may feel that because he works a job that he should be able to chalk that up to having all of his work done for the day when he comes home and expects a little grateful remuneration (if you know what I mean) in return at any time he wants it. A Woman works (at home or in the workplace) and shuffles the kids around between meal preparation and feels that she is owed a little conversation after the kids go to bed that doesn't include *Barney* or the *Power Rangers*. Both of them have placed a value on their work and most of the time each feels that they are the major contributor to making the home work. Both of you need to stop this *selfish kind* of thinking. Each party needs to stop thinking of themselves as the only giver in the family. You are one of two givers… and one of two receivers. Your job is not to find equitability, but rather to see how much you can bless each other for each others work.

We survey people about their private sex lives, and write manuals based on data gained by watching people perform sex in a laboratory setting. To junior high students we teach details of sexuality forbidden to previous generations. At the same time, I know of no greater failure among Christians than in presenting a persuasive approach to sexuality. Outside the church, people think of God as the great spoilsport of human sexuality, not its inventor. –Philip Yancey

My wife would be quick to point out that she is sick of female comedians parading around the idea that Women don't like sex and Men like it too much. She would quickly tell you that Women who have not been mistreated in this area, abused, or used, like it as much as a Man. Sex, as I said before is a good thing. God created it to be enjoyed by both parties. I believe our problems develop in the way Men have approached sex. Most Men approach sex as *Larry the Cable Guy... you know... Get'r Done!* Is it any wonder that this spouse, who speaks a different dialect, also approaches sex from a different perspective. For a Woman, great sex begins when the couple converses in the morning and culminates in a mutually satisfying orgasmic experience later that evening when the kids have gone to bed. Can I say the word *foreplay* without anyone freaking out? Too many Men see *foreplay* as the time it takes to get their work clothes off. Women on the other hand are looking for emotional intimacy to coincide with physical intimacy. The full book contains more about this than you really wanted to know. So let me just wrap it up with a challenge to the Men. If you are a two-minute sprinter... STOP! We are not at the Daytona Speedway. This is your *beloved*... let the time you take with her tell her that honest truth... in your words, in your time, and in your tender caresses. *Did you know that Women love to be hugged?*

> **Before marriage a Man will lie awake at night thinking about something you said; after marriage he will fall asleep before you finish saying it.**
> **–Helen Rowland**

If you really want to have a great sex life within a great marriage you need to eliminate all pornography from your line of sight. No person can live up to what twelve script writers, five camera angles, a *booty* double, and thousands of dollars of silicone can produce. Now when I say pornography I am not limiting that to internet nudity. The daytime soaps, the chick flicks, and the romance novels can be as detrimental to a females sex life as the girly magazines are to a male. Anything that makes your sex life a *comparative act* is going to cost you more than you want to pay. Is it any wonder that we are not sexually satisfied when we have been sexually snacking all day long. Great sex begins with exclusivity of the mind. Great sex continues as two people can experience and grow together without the aide of external arousal. I would challenge both sexes to go on a fast from [all] external sexual stimuli and see if that doesn't greatly improve their sex life. Enough said... read the whole book.

> **The quarrels of lovers are like summer storms. Everything is more beautiful when they have passed. –Suzanne Necker**

Every relationship has its fights. The problem is that most spouses fight more *against* their spouse than they fight *for* the marriage. Commit yourself to fighting FOR your marriage. Now when you fight - fight fair! The unacceptable fighting is that which is dealt in covert blows, underhanded responses, and loud apathy. It is what we in the field call *passive aggressiveness.* Quickly defined it would be acting poorly toward your spouse in an effort to express your anger rather than simply dealing openly and honestly with the issues. This is a big problem. It rips at the very soul of relationships. Be a Man, be a Woman, deal with your problems face to face and quit firing mortar into each others camp. The truth is you are in the same camp... and those mortars are killing both your marriages, because it is one and the same.

> **Opinions are like hind quarters, everybody has them, and many of them stink.**

Everybody can tell you what you need to "say" to your spouse, or what you need to do to get them to change. Most of these people have more problems than you. *We all like to be the expert on something… heck anything… everything!* I know - I know - here I am writing a book of my opinions. Get marital advice from people who have great marriages, and have had them for a long time. The girls down at the office or the boys at work need to get their own marriages in order. Why listen to them? If you are going to get help, find a godly professional who still believes the Bible truths offer more insight than Freudian bull droppings that blame everything on a perverted attraction to ones mother. *C'mon people… this aint rocket science here.* You wouldn't take your child's broken arm to a plumber, or would you? Well at least not unless that plumber also went to medical school. Mine did. *Who knew?*

> **There is no remedy for love but to love more.**
> **–Henry David Thoreau**

There is a final critical key ingredient to experiencing a lifelong great marriage. That is *forgiveness*. Marriages need *forgiveness* to reign freely because we are all jaded hurtful people at times. We all make mistakes and sometimes willfully decide to participate in actions that cause others pain. God has called every Christ follower to exemplify the same level of *forgiveness* He offered us in Christ Jesus our Lord. We need to model that forgiveness in our marriages as well as every other relationship in our lives. We need to model that whether or not the offending party asks for it, desires it, or deserves it. *Forgiveness* is as much about *our own* wholeness as it is about *our spouses* wholeness. *Unforgiveness* is a cancer that eats at our very soul. Keep it in you very long and you will wind up dead… and in a place where you really don't want to be. That is Biblical! So Ladies get your panties unwadded and get in there and fight *for* your marriage with everything that is in you. This means you will start with yourself. Men… you may be the lord of your castle, but remember your castle sits on land borrowed from the King of the universe. You are a master under the Master… live with that understanding. *Marriage is designed to be - Man living for the Woman and the Woman living for the Man.* We must call a moratorium on the "eye for an eye - tooth for a tooth" responses we have been giving to each other. Those who allow this in their marriage wind up blind and toothless. Stop it right here and right now. *Nobody pee'd in either of your Cheerios!*

This synopsis will now end where the larger book begins. With the *miracle of marriage* verse given by Jesus himself. This miracle can be yours. For the sake of your own happiness and the happiness of your spouse it must be attained.

> **Haven't you read in your Bible that the Creator originally made Man and**
> **Woman for each other, male and female? And because of this, a Man leaves**
> **father and mother and is firmly bonded to his wife, becoming one flesh - no**
> **longer two bodies but one. –Matthew 19:4-5**

Remember that only success stories become movies. Build a life and a marriage that becomes a legacy. Building a legacy takes work. You have what it takes. Your marriage will either be a great source of encouragement for your children or a sad memory. The choice is almost entirely up to you. Now don't be a lazy slug. Go back and read the book in its entirety. You will laugh, you will cry, and if you follow the principles given, you will wind up with a great marriage to boot! Leave a great marital legacy! You can. I believe in you.